FOREWORD BY **REBECCA ST. JAMES**

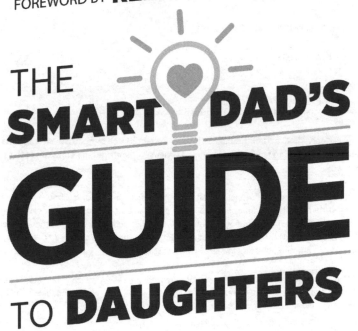

THE
SMART DAD'S
GUIDE
TO DAUGHTERS

> **101 REAL-WORLD TIPS** <
TO IMPROVE YOUR RELATIONSHIP—
AND SAVE YOUR SANITY

JESS MACCALLUM
& DALE REEVES

SHILOH RUN

Praise for
The Smart Dad's Guide to Daughters

As a father to nineteen children (fourteen of them adopted), and fourteen grandchildren (and still counting), I am always on the lookout for books that will help men become all-star dads. Jess and Dale have a slam dunk with their *Smart Dad's Guide to Daughters*. If you want to know why you should take your daughter to the NCAA Final Four, this book is for you. It's a perfect combination of humor, hands-on help, and wise biblical counsel.
—PAT WILLIAMS, SENIOR VICE PRESIDENT, ORLANDO MAGIC AND AUTHOR OF *LEADERSHIP EXCELLENCE*

Man, what a great offering. Dale and Jess have hit a home run with this down-to-earth guide for dads. It's a book that manages to be both insightful *and* fun to read. Pick it up. Page through it. Put it into practice. Both you and your daughter will be glad you did.
—STEVEN JAMES, BESTSELLING AUTHOR OF THE *KING AND SINGULARITY*

Some guys view fatherhood as a chore. . .but Smart Dads don't. Some guys think frowning is a key parenting tool. . .but Smart Dads smile more than necessary. Most guys don't realize that today's simple joys create the happy childhood your daughter (and you) will remember tomorrow and forever. Thankfully, *The Smart Dad's Guide to Daughters* has figured that part out for you. Seriously, do yourself a favor and buy this book. Use it. Enjoy it. Share it. You, and your daughter, will be very glad you did.
—MIKE NAPPA, PUBLISHER, FAMILYFANS.COM "THE FREE E-MAGAZINE FOR PARENTS"

This little book full of short, easy-to-read chapters is *huge*! I've never read a parenting book so jam-packed with helpful, practical wisdom and ideas—valuable insights that Jess and Dale learned in the trenches of raising their own daughters. You won't be able to implement all the ideas, but if you put even a handful of these into practice, you—and the daughter you deeply love—will be blessed! Thanks, guys, for this treasure chest!
—KURT JOHNSTON, HUSBAND, DAD, AUTHOR, YOUTH PASTOR AT SADDLEBACK CHURCH

When my precious daughter was born twenty years ago she didn't come with an instruction manual. I needed this book back then, but it is just as valuable today. If you have a daughter of any age, read this book and share it with a friend. I have known Dale Reeves for over twenty years. He is authentic, vulnerable, insightful, and funny—my kind of author. Enjoy!

—TROY JUSTICE, SENIOR DIRECTOR OF NBA'S INTERNATIONAL BASKETBALL OPERATIONS

Jess and Dale had me at the table of contents. In a world that sends mixed messages to women, these dads have given us a script for the most important voice in a daughter's life. Indispensible, no matter which stage of parenting you find yourself in.

—BETH GUCKENBERGER, AUTHOR, SPEAKER, FOUNDER OF BACK2BACK MINISTRIES

Parenting is hard. There is no pre-scripted instructional manual to follow. All we really have to fall back on is the grace of God and the collective wisdom of parents who have gone before us. Jess and Dale have a gem here—practical, simple suggestions on how dads can love their daughters better. And to top it off, it's a fun read.

—JOE BOYD, AUTHOR AND PRESIDENT OF REBEL PILGRIM PRODUCTIONS

As a father of two daughters, I've often wondered, *Why don't daughters come with an instruction manual?* Well, in *The Smart Dad's Guide to Daughters,* I found the next best thing (besides the Bible, of course). No joke! This book is witty, practical, full of wisdom, and a great resource for any father serious about having meaningful and unique connections with the daughters God has given him to raise.

—ARRON CHAMBERS, PASTOR AND AUTHOR OF *DEVOTED: ISN'T IT TIME TO FALL MORE IN LOVE WITH JESUS*

As a father of young daughters, my eyes misted up repeatedly while reading Jess and Dale's 101 real-world tips. Amazingly, they get me . . .and my girls! Their brotherly encouragement gave me three things every dad needs: permission to be affectionate, practical tips for expressing that affection, and a greater vision for what that affection accomplishes. I'm more convinced than ever that one of the greatest marks I can make on the world is raising confident women of God—one micro-date at a time.

—NOEL BOUCHÉ, PRESIDENT OF PUREHOPE

> CONTENTS <

CAN YOU SAY *GAWKY*?

CREATURE FROM ANOTHER PLANET

DARN, SHE'S BASICALLY A WOMAN

> FOREWORD <

One of my most precious memories from childhood involves my dad. I must have been eleven or twelve at the time. We went on a father-daughter date to see Amy Grant in concert in Sydney, Australia, where we lived. At the time, I had no idea I would follow in Amy's footsteps by becoming a Christian music artist! I remember scurrying down the street to the show, wanting to keep up with Dad's long legs. I held onto his hand as we approached the huge concert venue. It was so exciting to be there with him, to have his undivided attention that sweet evening. That night, I was a princess, and my dad was showing me, in a unique way, that I was special and dearly loved.

Not too long after that, I remember saying something very heartfelt to my dad. We were outside near the vegetable garden, and I looked up at him and said, "Dad, when I grow up, I want to marry someone like you!" Quality time, affirmation, making me feel important and valued—all these things were coming into play in those youthful moments with my dad. Times like these are so very instrumental in a young girl's life. They help lay a foundation for the way she will view herself, view men, and expect to be treated by a man. They also tremendously affect how she views her Father God.

The book you are about to read is incredibly important. I know that many men feel intimidated at times in parenting a daughter, especially as she grows up and begins looking and acting more like a young woman than a young girl.

> This is a book of encouragement for dads.

> It is a book that I know my husband will want to read now that we have a daughter!

> It is a book for every father who desires to connect in meaningful and unique ways with his daughter.

One of the authors of this book, Dale Reeves, is a man I know very well. I've had the privilege of writing several books with him since I was seventeen years old. He is a man of God, with a wonderful family, and so much wisdom to share. I'm thrilled that he and Jess MacCallum have written such a treasure as this book is! May God speak into your life and encourage and enhance your relationship with your little girl, who, in your heart, will always be so—no matter how old she gets.

Be blessed!

Rebecca St. James

Now to him who is able to do immeasurably more than all we ask or imagine, according to his power that is at work within us, to him be glory.
EPHESIANS 3:20–21 NIV

We are qualified to write a book on daughters because we both have been voted Father of the Year—in our respective homes—*every* year we've been eligible. The contest is local and is open to as many qualified voters as there are in the house. My (Jess's) son, for example, is ineligible to vote, because being a boy, he would cast his ballot for anyone—perhaps even a total stranger—in exchange for merely a free rental from Redbox. My girls, on the other hand, think I'm great, and that is what gets me to work on Monday mornings and makes me bite my tongue when they want to watch the Disney Channel instead of ESPN.

My (Dale's) girls are a bit older now—in their twenties—but they still love for me to take them to Disney movies. Yes, it's true. Not too long ago, the three of us sat and watched *Beauty and the Beast*—in 3D, complete with the glasses—alongside and in front of many snickering children. But as a bonus, due to many strategic partnerships with my girls throughout the years, it is now a realistic possibility for ESPN to be included in the channel mix—especially when the Cincinnati Bengals are in contention for winning their division. . .which is about once every ten years.

Girls are tricky creatures, fun and vexing. They experience life in ways that boys and dads just don't. Even when we see something of ourselves in our girls, it's always skewed by that chromosomal difference. Things you *think* you understood about them yesterday have already expired today.

Fortunately, we both have very patient daughters and wonderfully instructive wives (just one wife apiece), who have all helped us along the way to our becoming decent fathers. They have given us such incredible support that we felt compelled to write some of it down. But not in any *authoritative* way. These are more a collection of meditations, like Blaise Pascal's *Pensées,* only ours are about daughters—their joys, idiosyncrasies, and hormonal mood swings—rather than the easier topics that Pascal tackled, such as philosophy, theology, and mathematics.

Each daughter is unique—even if most dads are yawningly predictable—so we leave it to you to tailor these ideas to your own girl (or girls) as suits your situation. You may laugh at our misguided attempts at heroic feats, but we invite you to steal from the brilliant ideas that actually worked. Most of all, we encourage you to keep your own notebook; this list is just the beginning.

We have arranged the chapters chronologically, so you can decide how you'd like to digest this book. These sections include Little Princess (preschool); Can You Say *Gawky*? (elementary age); Creature From Another Planet (teenage years); and Darn, She's Basically a Woman (late high school, college, and beyond). Or you can just plow through the chapters one at a time, dog-ear what you need, and ignore (or learn from) the mistakes we've made along the way.

You will notice more entries in the Little Princess section than in any other. That just means you should get started on some of these things sooner rather than later. Many of the things that apply to your little princess will apply to her later in life, as well. So, we recommend that you start reading in the first section and go the distance.

We're so glad you're part of our tribe! We wish you and your girls many blessings along the way.

Jess MacCallum & Dale Reeves

> LITTLE PRINCESS <

1. BE UNAPOLOGETICALLY MASCULINE

The way God designed women is amazing, annoying, and attractive all at the same time. You begin to see these traits at a very early age. Women are most definitely not the same as men. That's good news—it means we have something to offer. The gift we enjoy called *masculinity* is essential for establishing your daughter's female identity. I mean, how else will your little pumpkin understand the meaning of the word *gross* if you don't define it for her regularly? Or how will she know which cologne smells manly for her future husband if she hasn't smelled her dad after a day of yard work?

Seriously, your masculinity is a gift for the women in your life. It's like a magic mirror that shows them their femininity. They find security in it, even if it sometimes comes in a stinky package. Your ways will be funny and mysterious and appalling to them, but they will delight in laughing at you among themselves. That's what they do. When you wonder why they are giggling behind your back, that's probably it—your *hairy* back.

Stuff like wearing your T-shirt as a nightgown, watching you shave, and rubbing your bald spot are milestones your daughters will never forget.

Be masculine; your daughter will feel comforted. Be strong; she will feel protected. Be aggressive; she will feel valuable. Always be sensitive to her differences, but never feel awkward about yours.

"I am going the way of all the earth.
Be strong, therefore, and show yourself a man."
1 KINGS 2:2

These were the heads of their fathers' households. . .mighty men
of valor, famous men, heads of their fathers' households.
1 CHRONICLES 5:24

THINK ABOUT IT. . .

- Not every man will be a warrior or a hero to the world, but every dad is a hero to his little princess.

- God made men and women different to be complementary; the Fall created friction between those differences.

- We are not to erase our differences, no matter what the social engineers might say. On the contrary, we are to celebrate them and reclaim them.

2. PLAY DRESS-UP

There may very well be exceptions to the following discussion, but because I have boringly stereotypical gender roles in my family, I can't advise you on the issue of playing dress-up if your son loves Broadway musicals and your daughter prefers Resident Evil 4.

Generally speaking, girls have more nuanced imaginations than boys. They actually create things without planning to destroy them immediately after completion. They develop entire worlds of play by the age of two and a half. And they understandably expect to be center stage with a supporting cast—and with you included. They have roles in mind that require a strong male lead, and you are the first choice of the casting department. I understand that many dads want to play dress-up about as much as a cat wants a bath, but if *I* can sit through a tea party, any man can. The satisfying payoff is making the event come alive for your little sweetie and an audience of stuffed animals.

Being a good costar when your daughter is young will prepare you for the supporting role you will play in the future, as well: a little in the background, stage left (with a big friggin' sword), ready to rescue the damsel if she gets into distress. That's a part that will last in her mind a lot longer than you might imagine.

THINK ABOUT IT. . .

- ☼ Playing dress-up is, more often than not, a female pasttime. That means you are stepping into her world when you do it.

- ☼ Dressing up with what she chooses lets her be in charge.

- ☼ Take pictures of the event for her to remember the fun you had.

TAKING INVENTORY

> Many times, dress-up is a spontaneous request. When can you make time during the week to just spend time playing with your daughter?

> Does your daughter play any dress-up games on a regular basis? Is she a Cinderella girl? A Pocahontas type? A tea-time hostess?

3. BE CONFIDENT IN YOURSELF FOR HER SAKE

Confident people make history. Good and bad history, I'll grant you, but they make it for a reason. Most people are looking for a leader, a star to steer by, if you will. Even leaders are looking for leaders. And what sets most leaders apart is self-confidence.

Now, if you're not brimming with this quality, there's still some good news. You are Daddy to your little princess, and you're bigger than she is. That's an immediate blessing to get us rolling. Your daughter looks up to you both physically and figuratively. Of course, as she grows up, she needs more than a hulking presence in the background. But starting with her natural awe of you at least gives you time to work on becoming more confident, decisive, and consistent. You don't have to swagger or wear a uniform, but it wouldn't hurt to stand up straight, believe in something bigger than yourself, and communicate your convictions with some authority. Some men confuse this with raising their voice. Confident people know to lower their voices.

Confidence is a universally appealing trait, unless you mix it with arrogance. Fortunately, God invented humiliation to balance the scales, and He will apply it liberally to your life and mine when needed.

One more thing. Confident dads don't work through their personal fears and issues in front of an audience. It may have worked for troubled characters like Hamlet, but daughters want a safe harbor. You can project confidence even when you're afraid or unsure—CEOs and politicians do it all the time. Save your indecision for the Chinese buffet and your deepest fears for your accountant. Your daughter will find rest in your self-confidence.

THINK ABOUT IT. . .

- Is there any trait more appealing in a leader than confidence? (Yeah, yeah, I know. . .justice, mercy, insight, etc. But those are hard to see until the situation arises.)

- Confidence isn't loud or bombastic or arrogant. Those are signs of insecurity. A non-anxious presence is far more compelling.

- A girl has a lot coming at her these days. A solid, steady father will be a treasure for her entire life.

TAKING INVENTORY

> Do you have an outlet for yourself? Someone who will let you drop your guard so you can get a balanced view of things? This is essential for you to be healthy and give your girl what she needs.

> Have you developed any habits that show you are not confident in yourself? Drink too much? Curse at inanimate objects? Road rage? We all have habits that come from a lack of self-confidence—so let's start together to look at those "billboards" of ourselves and take them down.

4. DON'T UNDERESTIMATE YOUR SYMBOLISM

Not that any man deserves it, but your little princess is going to put you on a pedestal. Crazy, scary—even laughable, I know; but you and I are *automatically* awesome to our girls. And considering the reactions we usually evoke, that's pretty cool.

Before the sheer magnitude of this misplaced worship crushes your brain, let me assure you that it's good for her—as long as you and I don't try to stay there. We dads represent the first impressions of God to our kids, and then we have the privilege of helping them transfer those attachments to God Himself. But as you come down to earth, don't underestimate the power of what you symbolize—something larger, stronger, and more secure than any mere man. The way you smell, the way you dress, the way you cough or sneeze—as repellent as some of those traits might be to your friends and coworkers—can be funny and warm symbols for your daughter. Girls are little touchy-feely creatures. My youngest loves to borrow my T-shirts to sleep in. I never refuse her, no matter what. She is wrapping herself in her daddy. I want to create *afterimages* for when she is grown and on her own. *Remembering* is part of our identity, and identity is reinforced by symbols of attachment.

The great thing about symbols is that some of the most meaningful ones for my daughters are almost effortless for me—things like my bald head, my nightstand items, my favorite movie. Sometimes we can help our daughters without ever leaving our overstuffed easy chairs.

A WORD FROM THE WORD

Now listen, Joshua the high priest, you and your friends who are sitting in front of you—indeed they are men who are a symbol, for behold, I am going to bring in My servant the Branch.

ZECHARIAH 3:8

You know what kind of men we proved to be among you for your sake.

1 THESSALONIANS 1:5

OUR TRANSLATION

> You are bigger than yourself when God decides you are. And He decided it when you had kids.

THINK ABOUT IT. . .

- Being a symbol of something larger than ourselves is about as easy as it's going to get. Just don't get in the way!

- Keep an eye out for small, important things your daughter likes about you. Things you can set aside, or gift to her when she's older. Nothing will be more meaningful to her than something with warm, happy memories of you.

5. CREATE THEME NIGHTS

A girl's imagination is staggeringly detailed. Costumes, lighting, and sound all make the experience more real. Give my son a stick and he has everything he needs to storm the beaches of Normandy or bring down the Tokugawa Shogunate. My little girls want scenery. They love full costuming, complete with coiffure, and preferably enough time to get ready (because *anticipation* is part of the whole experience). That's what I love about "theme night" with my daughters. It gives them time to enjoy the event well before it happens. For example, a medieval theme (also known as Knight Night) is good for two days' worth of planning and fun. The last time we did this, I wore my kilt (*yes*, Scottish DNA always looks for an opportunity) and we roasted "wild game." Actually, it was New York strip, but to me New York is pretty wild. If you are a deer hunter, this should be a real win-win.

Of course, my daughters already own a number of princess gowns, hats, slippers, etc. My wife managed a promising wench costume (and promised to wear it again later) and we watched Disney's *Four Musketeers*. I realize that Athos, Porthos, Aramis, and D'Artagnan aren't technically medieval, but we'll correct that misconception before the girls take their all-important SATs.

The point is to come up with something better for Friday nights than, "I dunno, what do *you* want to do?" That is an evening killer no matter what age a girl is! Other themes you can try include Samurai Night, Cowboy Night, Hawaiian Night, or Fashion Night. Some of these will depend on what's in your daughter's dress-up bin. Or your own tolerance for humiliation. Get into it with your little princess, and become part of her imagination forever.

THINK ABOUT IT. . .

- Nothing says "you're important" quite like planning ahead.

- Young kids, especially girls, live in their imagination. A theme night gives you and your princess a chance to have an adventure in her world.

TAKING INVENTORY

> Is there a costume or party store near your house? (Just walking around in there will give you ideas.)

> Does she have a favorite movie that you could turn into a fun night together by dressing the parts?

> Ask your daughter: If you could have lived in any other time, what would it be?

6. GET A MAKEOVER

One night, I found myself watching my daughters and a friend (all between the ages of eight and eleven) while my son was spending the night out and my wife was just out spending. The little ladies' Friday night had been thoroughly planned for days. Our house was now a spa and they were rich celebrities. That meant bathrobes, hair in towels, slippers, and a full manicure and facial. In case you've never paid much attention to skin care, a facial for spa-celebrity-spend-the-nights includes a mud mask and cucumber slices on your eyelids. As it happens, the mud mask is about the same color green as the cucumbers—and don't tell me it wasn't *planned* that way.

While the celebrities lounged in the den, away from the paparazzi (me), ate confectionary delights from the in-house baker (also me), and waited for the butler (me again) to check on their next whim, I snuck away to the bathroom to transform myself into a celebrity. I applied the mud mask, leaving large areas around the eyes, and carefully sliced my own cuke sunglasses. I sauntered into the lounge area to great squeals of delight as they had begun snacking on their vegetable eye care products. (Where the heck is that butler anyway? I need a drink with my cucumbers.)

Nothing gets a dad into his daughter's inner circle quite like sharing in her whimsical, feminine world. And sometimes you get great skin at the same time.

Spa Celebrity Night is not for every guy. I know that. I just did it on a whim, and the results were fantastic. Making their fun evening even more fun was the point. But getting to that point meant I had to do something really silly, and honestly, a bit awkward. *C'est la vie!* Fun is fun wherever you find it. If you can't bring yourself to slap on the mud mask, then at least let the girls curl or straighten your hair. That's not an option for me. I'm bald.

7. TAKE HER TO WORK WHEN YOU'RE NOT SCHEDULED TO BE THERE

My daughters always like to go to my office. Usually that's challenging, because I manage a large printing company—and the only thing more hectic than an average day at work is outright tribal warfare. Scheduling conflicts, sales problems, equipment breakdowns, and client alterations constantly interrupt my YouTube viewing, much less leave me time to show my daughters what I do! So I've gotten to where I bring them to the office after work or on weekends. Then I can answer all their questions, untangle my paper clips, collect all their drawings, and have a relaxed time with them.

For girls, a trip to the office is like a field trip into Daddy's world. They don't necessarily understand that much, but being the sensitive beings they are, they want a *feel* for where Daddy is when he's not at home. It certainly holds more mystery and excitement for them than for most of us.

THINK ABOUT IT. . .

- Your work is a mystery to your little ones. An occasional visit to your office is a chance for them to feel included in something that's important to you.

- You may need to get your employer's permission, but very few will decline, unless you work at a nuclear facility, the morgue, or Area 51.

- Meeting people you work with gives your girl a chance to meet "Daddy's friends." And girls understand the world through relationships more than anything else.

8. TEACH HER A "BOYS" SPORT

I know I'm in the minority when football season starts. Not only am I *not aware* it has started, I can't name an NFL team other than the Dallas Cowboys—and them only because their cheerleaders are permanently embedded in the seventh-grade layer of my brain. I never played competitive sports outside of gym class and instead gravitated toward weight training, rock climbing, and martial arts. In all of these endeavors, I am unquestionably average or below, but without a team to let down when I peel off the wall or tap out on the mat. (Yes, I know, "Jesus didn't tap out!") Despite this "handicap" (I'm not a golfer either), I actually coached my youngest daughter's soccer team when she was four. Thankfully, as long as you can yell louder than both teams, and remember it's all about feet, you're qualified.

Despite my own limitations, I have offered my girls the chance to try everything. Especially things that do not traditionally have high female participation: rock climbing, judo, trail running, weight lifting, to name a few. My eldest even tried paintball. She quit when she got hit the first time, but at least she tried! That's my point. There shouldn't be an intimidation factor for girls who want to be athletic. Competition is life. Don't let your girl be squeezed into a mold just because "she's a girl."

THINK ABOUT IT. . .

- Find a successful female coach or athlete and make an appointment for your daughter to meet her and discuss options.

- Make a date to try new sports—a Saturday at the driving range, batting cage, or skateboard park can shed new light on her interests.

- Look ahead at ESPN's schedule for any upcoming events that show women branching out. (But not beach volleyball; no man's daughter should be playing beach volleyball.)

9. GIVE EACH OTHER NICKNAMES

Nicknames are perhaps the most universal sign of affection. I'm talking about the kind the other person accepts—not ones like Toad, Wart, or Crusty. Fond nicknames are like secret identities shared by a select few. It's almost inevitable you will come up with several options when your daugher is a baby, because parents just automatically coo and chatter over litle girls. In my family, we've made up and forgotten dozens over the years, but the ones that stick are the ones the girls know themselves by. One that stuck was Scoops (shortened from "scoops of love" because she was tiny for so long that you could scoop her up with one hand), and Clooney Bear (a play on her middle name, Claire). Now, I have just broken the fundamental rule of pet names by telling you what they are. They're meant to be used by the inner circle only. But for illustration purposes I have chosen to reveal them here, and I will pay an expensive price at the mall to obtain forgiveness. (See my later chapter on the healing power of mall trips.)

Don't forget that these names run both ways. You will need one if you don't already have one. I am Dad-O-Man. I'd like to think it's a superhero derivative, but it's more likely akin to Cash-O-Matic. In any case, don't let your daughter down. You can stand to be called some pretty silly stuff if it means making a lifelong connection with her.

*He appointed the twelve: Simon (to whom He gave the name Peter),
and James, the son of Zebedee, and John the brother of James
(to them He gave the name Boanerges, which means,
"Sons of Thunder").*
Mark 3:16–17

OUR TRANSLATION

Apparently, there were a lot of nicknames in Jesus' day. You'd have to ask a historian why, but even among the apostles there was Simon the Zealot; Thomas, called Didymus (the twin); Matthew, also known as Levi; Bartholomew, called Nathanel. . .you get the picture. The most interesting thing is that Jesus only gave nicknames to three: Peter, James, and John. These three became his inner circle. They were the only ones present at his Transfiguration (Mark 5:37) and Paul later called them the "pillars" of the church (Galatians 2:9).

What does this have to do with daughters? Well, my own conclusion is simply that familiarity and affection breed trust.

TAKING INVENTORY

> If you don't already use a term of endearment with your little princess, you may want to test the waters on a few possibilities.

> If you're calling her something she doesn't like, stop it and find something else. Duh.

> Some girls don't like being called by their nicknames in front of their friends, so make sure you get permission.

10. TAKE HER TO THE MALL TO SHOP

For me, the mall is a four-letter word. In fact, it comes from the same Latin root as the word for *hell*. But, for girls, the mall is heaven on earth, especially as they head into the teen years. I'm sure it's tied to the girlish need to "see and be seen." My daughters spend as much time getting ready to go as they will actually spend at the mall. For me, going to the mall is an endurance test with the occasional oasis of Starbucks or the Sears tool department. Except the reason you go with your daughter will probably exclude tools. Thankfully, you can share a mocha-frappa-something and sit down and talk.

Your girl will like a lot of things you don't. There's no better way to tell her she's important than to go with her into the lion's den of materialism and hormone-laced ostentation. And it's best that you and I know what's coming: One day she'll be old enough to be [gasp] *dropped off* at the mall! While secretly rejoicing that you don't have to go anymore, your thoughts will be disturbed by the images of her wandering with her friends in the boy-infested waters that surround the Hollister store. Having taken her through these straits before, you will be better prepared to let her go, or forbid it, whichever you feel is best.

In any case, she will remember the day you took her to ten stores, bought nothing but socks and hair bows, ate lunch, rode the carousel, and just listened to her talk about girl stuff. For a girl, there's nothing like it. For you and me. . .if we're lucky Sears will one day relocate the tool department next to missy fashions.

THINK ABOUT IT. . .

 Anytime you can build a memory on your daughter's "turf," you build your relationship for later. You may not have the same sense of dread I do about the mall—I certainly like to go into Starbucks and Williams-Sonoma. Maybe you're lucky enough to have a mall nearby with rides, or a skating rink, or an arcade. In any case, the mall trip is an easy way to spend an afternoon together, rain or shine.

11. WASH, DRY, AND COMB HER HAIR

Girls have a thing about hair that goes deeper than anything a boy understands, except for maybe a few senators and congressmen. Back in the days when I had hair, it mattered how it looked. Nowadays I just put to death the few survivors of the whole treacherous bunch. . .but I digress.

My daughters have had their feminine identity wrapped up in their hair since they began noticing they had hair. Women's hair is a historic and cultural phenomenon worldwide, and that does not exclude your house or mine. To affirm that your baby girl is beautiful and girly, you can hardly do more good than to wash her hair, dry it, and comb it out. Through this exercise, you express a tenderness and an acclaim of value that words could never produce. For your little girl, it will also tell her she's beautiful, and worth the time to be taken care of. Really, considering it's a part of routine personal hygiene, you're getting an awesome return for the simplest effort. And you'll get bonus points with your wife, who will get the night off!

THINK ABOUT IT. . .

 This is a very practical opportunity to continue to give your daughter appropriate physical touches. It takes time and gentleness, and you can't go wrong with either one of those when your daughter is little. Try making George Washington hair with a Moses beard— it takes some skill. Besides, it won't be long before she outgrows shampoo sculptures and bubbly beards.

12. PAINT HER TOENAILS

Painting toenails is a uniquely girlie activity. It is one of those details about being a girl that has no equivalent in the masculine world, no counterbalance, no frame of reference. We just don't do anything quite so colorful and meticulous and chemical. Men can be fussy about their hair or clothes, but that's just amateur stuff compared to makeup and nails. This gives you a spot to connect to your daughter's world in a special way. To serve in a way that is all about her being a girl.

Before my wife and I bought our daughters real nail paint, they colored their fingers and toes with markers and white-out. They are wired to be girls. So, when they were old enough, we got the sparkly nail paint that's made for kids and silly people. They learned with amazing speed to paint ambidextrously. They did a decent job on their fingernails, but painting toes can be awkward when you're tiny—so this became an opportunity to give them a little attention. Go for it. If you can stand the smell of the polish, you will have a funny and memorable evening.

THINK ABOUT IT. . .

- Painting her nails will only work when your little one is, well, little. So your window of opportunity is small. Don't miss it.

- It's been a long time since my girls were young enough for me to do this, but the time or two I did, they thought it was hilarious. I sat on the floor and put a towel under their feet, and pretended to be French. (No offense to French men, it just seemed like someone who did it for a living would be French.)

13. TEACH HER "THE FALLING GAME" TO BUILD TRUST

Okay, this one has a very real physical requirement. *Do not* do this exercise if there's any chance you'll throw out your back. The whole point of the falling game is that it's *falling*, not *impacting*. It's an old hippy generation team-building exercise that is only fun these days for people under twelve years old.

Here's how it works: Your daring little princess stands with her back to you, her big, strong, trustworthy daddy. She extends her arms and falls backward and you catch her before she hits the ground. Got it? *Before* she hits the ground. If you ever screw this one up, you'll be rebuilding her trust for years. But if you get it right, it will be your daughter who learns to let go and trust you.

My youngest loves this game, and I have developed the ability to catch her at the very last possible second. Sometimes she steps backward instinctively, but that's the fun. It's like so much of life—it depends on the day. Ultimately it's a way she can let herself go and fall into her daddy's arms, and you'll have gained an inner trust factor—something that will go a long way when she's older and hitting the ground is more of a metaphor, but a much harsher reality.

THINK ABOUT IT. . .

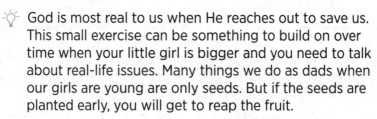 God is most real to us when He reaches out to save us. This small exercise can be something to build on over time when your little girl is bigger and you need to talk about real-life issues. Many things we do as dads when our girls are young are only seeds. But if the seeds are planted early, you will get to reap the fruit.

14. TAKE HER SHOPPING FOR A SPECIAL DRESS— JUST THE TWO OF YOU

I was trained to hate the ladies department by being dragged along on shopping trips by my mother. For years, I was bored out of my mind and embarrassed beyond measure at the same time. (I finally put my foot down last week and told her I'd wait for her at the food court.)

Most men aren't patient waiters in any case—at least not without a television nearby. So the combination of the endless non-adventure of watching your wife try on item after item and being deprived of your cable connection does not make this an easy task. But, and I emphasize *but*, when it comes to your daughter, it's an outing worth the Herculean effort. I've found it works best between the time she realizes she's a girl and when she realizes she's a woman. Somewhere between the ages of eight and thirteen.

Once her figure starts to pop out and her friends' opinions become more important than yours, you'll be safely ignored in the shopping ritual. But before that happens, you can bless your little one with the self-confidence that can only come from her daddy. Pick a day when you won't be rushed—'cause that would ruin the effect. She will already know of about five stores she'll want to go to, and you should plan for lunch as well. You don't have to get the special dress for a special occasion, but that would be an added bonus.

THINK ABOUT IT. . .

☼ It's an evolving world for girls at this age—an exciting and scary one. Any transition time in a girl's life needs a stabilizing force. Here is an easy chance for you to be that. Your girl is listening for voices that confirm she is feminine and beautiful. Yours, believe it or not, is the loudest voice she will hear. And if you don't make your voice the loudest, she will find one to replace it.

TAKING INVENTORY

> For this to be a successful outing, you will likely need some expertise from outside your own experience. Get your wife to provide guidelines on stores, styles, sizes, colors, etc. (If you're a single dad, get input from women who dress well and have daughters.)

> Building a wardrobe is not your main goal, but it wouldn't hurt to buy stuff that matches what your daughter already has. Check her closet, ask you wife or other expert, and then consult your daughter. Ask her what's missing, so you have a target during the hunt.

> And for gosh sakes, take some pictures of the event for the memories!

15. TALK TO HER EVERY DAY, ESPECIALLY IF YOU TRAVEL

I can't explain what makes me so sought-after, besides good looks, a keen personality, and a vibrant sense of humor. Other than those, why would my little girl find me so interesting that a day without me makes her feel lost? Just a mystery for us dads to ponder until the teen years, when things slow down a bit.

But until I become obsolete, I understand that my little girls need to hear from me every day. Sound obvious? Considering how much stuff clamors for our unique and undivided attention, it may be something you and I need to tattoo to our wrists just beside our watches. That way the reminder to take time to talk to our girls will be there when we are rushing out the door in the morning, trying to catch the news, leaving for Wednesday night church, or gauging the time left till the game starts. However you choose to remind yourself, it would be the mistake of a lifetime to make your girl feel secondary when it comes to making time to really connect with her.

Girls are natural communicators, but not for the sake of merely exchanging information. Your attention matters. She's not even looking for your opinion necessarily, she just wants you to be interested in her.

THINK ABOUT IT...

☼ To succeed, shut up and listen. Your daughter will carry the conversation while you get all the points. Pursue her with open-ended questions, and follow up on her answers. If she isn't interested in talking right then, she'll let you know, and you can try again tomorrow.

TAKING INVENTORY

> Do you have any scheduling conflicts (military deployment, business travel, divorced, etc.) that would keep you from speaking to your daughter at least once a day?

> If you are restricted in your access to your daughter, and daily communication is not possible, then develop a schedule that will work and adhere to it religiously.

> Assuming you see your little girl daily, do you wait for her to initate conversation or do you ask her how her day was?

> Would you say you are approachable from her perspective, or will she be in therapy later working through how her dad was "never really there"?

16. DON'T BE AFRAID TO TALK GOOFY

I know how I talk to my girls when I think no one is listening, and it's ridiculous. I could write cartoon dialogue and do all the voices. I mean, I sound like someone used my brain's speech center for a med school demonstration. But it's fun and natural to me. Babbly silly talk starts when you have a baby, when it appears your language skills are temporarily at matching levels. But girls love this! Even as they get older, it gives them a sense of inner communication with the most opposite creature on two legs they encounter day to day. You and I, as dads, are the slightly dangerous beasts that our girls love to play with, flirt with, be scared of, and be comforted by.

The trick comes when a girl gets a little older and her friends (or worse, *your* friends) are around. Do you still give her the same silly good-bye voice that you do when no one is watching? Do you "act your age" or remember that it's *her* age that matters? And just wait until she gets old enough to call your cell phone. . .when you're surrounded by colleagues—tough ones who all played sports in college. And she wants to say good night like you do at home, the *normal*, silly way. It's a tough call.

When that happens, try to keep in mind that her comfort is paramount, and your discomfort will fade. And if your friends give you a hard time, just kiss them on the forehead and tell them they're being *cotton-headed ninny-muggins*.

> Do you really care what people outside your family think more than what your daughter appreciates?

> Before she was ready, did you do away with fun, silly things you enjoyed together, because you felt uncomfortable?

> To her friends, and age-mates, you are already pretty goofy, so what's the big deal?

17. ALWAYS KISS HER GOOD NIGHT

Above all, she's a girl, and you can't forget she wants your love and affection. Girls love consistency in their dads. My oldest (now twenty) actually has a sign over her door that says, "Always Kiss Me Goodnight." If I miss this for any reason, I get a smiling rebuke when she tracks me down asleep in front of the TV, or dozing book-faced in bed. The goodnight kiss is the final stamp of approval, no matter what things have transpired that day. It's the sweet exclamation point to a great day, or it's the everything-will-be-all-right-in-the-morning signal when it's been a tough day. This is the moment she is granted permission to fall asleep without anything edging its way between you two. It's an assurance to both of you of the permanence of love.

Girls are touchy-feely more often than not. I guess there are some exceptions, but I always wonder if they are exceptions who don't *want* to be. Is she really not interested in your affirmation from a kiss goodnight, or is she hurt and put off because of larger reasons? Have you left something to fester until it comes down to your being held at a distance? Have you not acclimated her to being affirmed with affection? Kissing your daughter goodnight, every night you are home, is the last gift of the day you can give her. Don't make excuses that she doesn't want you there, unless you need to deal with bigger issues first.

OUR TRANSLATION

> If ever there was a holy kiss, it should be from a dad to his kids. When we're appropriately affectionate with our kids, it builds our relationship with them on a firm foundation of peace and assurance.

BONUS THOUGHT

My dad was a veteran of World War II and not given to much conversation or affection—and yet even he kissed me and my sister goodnight every night! If John Wayne's long lost brother can do it, any man can.

18. APPLAUD HER THEATRICAL EFFORTS

It takes a lot of guts to get up on stage, even for adults. And many a delicate self-esteem has been crushed up there. Our little ones take a great risk to dance or sing or act or play the piano, and they deserve to have a cheering section. Your proud face may be the thing that gives your daughter the reassurance she needs to make it through.

If there's one thing all women share, it's the "total package" mentality. It isn't just a half-hour performance before you all go out for pizza, it's the crown jewel of months of hard work. Even women as small as your tiniest princess see life on a continuum. Her recital may be penciled into your calendar or smartphone between a morning meeting and a Wednesday church service, but to her it isn't a singular event. It has a long beginning, a highlight, and a *dénouement*, "a series of events that follow a dramatic or narrative climax, thus serving as the conclusion of the story. Conflicts are resolved, creating normality for the characters and a sense of catharsis, or release of tension and anxiety."[1]

This is how girls are programmed to see the world. So even though you think the event is over, it ain't over. Take the time your daughter needs to bring all the preparation and performance into perspective. Busy dads should make every effort to be at the recital, because daughters will most certainly weigh the choice to miss it on an unbalanced scale. If you do have to miss (and we all do at some time), the *dénouement* can work in your favor. You can still be involved by being genuinely interested, urging her to continue her art, asking for a private performance, or watching the event on video and asking her to narrate. Make sure she knows you

---

1. http://denouement.askdefine.com/

aren't "trying to make it up to her," because that puts a sense of obligation into the mix and would spoil her and give her a false sense of power. (Guilt is the gift that keeps on giving.) Above everything else, make sure to tell her that you're proud of her.

OUR TRANSLATION

> If the apostle Paul compared himself and his work to a father building up his kids, doesn't that mean we dads have a God-given power to encourage?

THINK ABOUT IT. . .

Long before your daughter gets up in front of dozens or hundreds of people, you and her mom are her audience. Just make sure that, when the stakes get higher, you match the moment with the level of your attention to her. Have flowers ready for her when her ballet is done, make reservations at her favorite restaurant, plan an after-party at your house, or turn the rest of the evening into a date night. She wants your affirmation and attention more than anyone else's.

19. TAKE HER TO A VALENTINE'S DAY LUNCH

My wife started this tradition for me several years ago. I take my daughters to lunch and my wife to dinner. The girls get dressed up, and it's pretty easy to get a reservation for lunch. I get them each a corsage (actually, my wife gets them so they can be refrigerated ahead of time), a card, and a present. They make me cards and off we go.

Every year, I try to do a different kind of restaurant or experience. One year, it was an underground gourmet eatery, and the next it was on top of the tallest building in our city (a mere twenty stories, but for them it might as well have been a hundred.) One year, I took them to a neighboring town with a bistro in a renovated nineteenth-century store. The attention we get is part of the experience as well. Folks stare (especially the moms), some comment, and everyone smiles. They see something that just doesn't happen much, even though planning and pulling off the event is about as easy as it gets. Maybe if more dads would try this there'd be more princesses in the world.

THINK ABOUT IT...

 We all know it: No holiday is more of a fake occasion than Valentine's Day. (Saint Valentine must cringe at the slander of his good name!) But that's the society we live in. One of the reasons I do a lunch with my daughters every year (even when they've had boyfriends) is to remind them that God's love is more valuable than any man's. And in the case that they don't have a special boy in their life, it protects them from the false belief that they're not loved.

20. SET A GOOD EXAMPLE

Isn't this idea about the most obvious thing you can think of? And maybe the hardest too. My daughters watch everything I do and say. All kids do—whether we dads are happy about it or not. And though they're not even conscious of it, they are creating a worldview from the things they take in. And they may eventually come to some very clear conclusions:

> If dad cusses at inanimate objects, then it must be okay.

> Treating mom like she's a dummy must mean women are dummies—so I must be one too.

> Watching reruns instead of talking with the family is because we're not that interesting.

Ouch. On the positive side of the equation, we dads have a unique opportunity to make better daughters for the world to appreciate. You can set standards in things like courtesy and respect, hard work and tenderness, that will force every boy who ever wants to impress your daughter to step up his game. By your good example, you will build an internal framework in your daughter for what a real man is supposed to be. She'll dismiss the losers without your having to tell her which ones those are, and without your having to clean your guns in the living room when she brings them over. She'll be a better woman for your being a better man.

THINK ABOUT IT. . .

How many bad examples have you had in your own life? Too many, right? Setting the right kind of example means that you parent based on who you are. Are you who you want to be? Even if no one was watching—but, believe me, they are—do you choose the healthier path and the wise solution? As clichéd as it sounds, *doing* the right thing is more powerful than *saying* the right thing.

21. ENCOURAGE DANCE AND THE ARTS

I don't know if it's possible for little girls *not* to dance. It seems they are outfitted with a motion sensor wired from the ears to their hips. My own girls remind me of the African tribe I heard about on NPR once that has only one word to describe both music and dance—there's no distinction in their world between the two. That's refreshing to me. Physical self-expression is good because there are parts of the brain that seem to reside in areas outside the skull—especially in the hands and feet. (I personally believe it's a modern phenomenon for boys to *avoid* dance. In my dad's day, an accomplished man could waltz and square dance as well as hunt, fish, and prepare his own taxes.)

Thankfully, girls are still encouraged to dance, by and large, and so my two took ballet and modern dance and had dance sleepovers, and generally learned that their bodies were good, and they could be feminine and graceful while still being modest. (Modesty should grow with age and self-awareness; little girls are exploring movement, older girls are exploring people's reactions to their movements. Keep an eye on that!) Also, make sure your house is "dance-proofed." At one dance party, my girls and a friend decided to execute a synchronized move that ended up pulling the mantel off the den wall.

Speaking of my house, it is also covered in paintings, drawings, sketches, sculptures, mobiles—you name it, there's art for it. (My son did one or two of these things, but they are restricted to his room due to the violent nature of the content and the excessive use of the color red.) Around the public areas of the house, my girls have a growing gallery.

Then, of course, there are the plays, the puppet theater, the musicals; singing with the chorus, their brother's band,

and solo events; guitar, piano, ukulele; pottery and basket weaving.

It's all about expressing themselves, and joining with God in the joy of creation. Encourage it.

OUR TRANSLATION

> God loves celebrating with dance and music. The arts are his creation and he lets us enjoy them along with him.

THINK ABOUT IT. . .

☼ Finding your daughter's niche may take some experimentation. But exposure to various kinds of dance and music is fun. You get to watch your girl learn and grow and find what she's good at. It may cost a little bit—dance lessons, guitars, a piano—but, in the end, you and she will be glad for the investment.

22. READ OR MAKE UP BEDTIME STORIES

There's a special time built into every day where a daddy can

> be the most magical person in the world

> be forgiven for whatever he did or didn't do

> learn what's really important to his daughter

> be reminded of what's really important in life

> give his wife the much-needed break she deserves

> all of the above

That special time is bedtime. Yes, that peculiar battleground of whether you really meant "nine o'clock, *or else*." The time when TV promises to deliver what it never has before—something well-written and original. The time when your work deadline becomes a living, breathing threat to humanity. Yep, bedtime.

As a printer, I love books, and as a writer, I like to make up stories. Bedtimes, hard as they might be, became my chance to share both with my girls. But most important, it was a quiet time of imagination that we shared. A time to teach the values I wanted them to have. And it was a time to just relax in each other's company.

So read stories. Or make them up. Thankfully, the standards of quality in my house were very low, so anything I said seemed to make the kids happy. Or maybe it was just that I took the time to do it. It's an opportunity almost every day, depending on your personal situation. Take advantage of it as often as you can. It will show up later in the quality of communication you have with your daughter when the time for bedtime stories has passed.

A WORD FROM THE WORD

"I will open My mouth in parables;
I will utter things hidden since the foundation of the world."
MATTHEW 13:35

OUR TRANSLATION

> Stories are memorable and powerful. They communicate truth while entertaining. No wonder storytelling is at the core of every culture, and why Jesus himself made it a part of his daily ministry.

23. PRAY WITH HER

It doesn't matter how little or much theology I know, praying is the simplest and toughest thing in my day. Not the desperate prayer for a solution at work or a parking space close to the mall's food court. Those flare-gun shots of petition I have honed to perfection. No, I'm talking about the purposeful prayer for someone you love who's listening and who hasn't a clue what religious words like *providence* and *sanctification* mean. I'm talking about asking for real blessings for a real girl who's sad about losing a shoe, or mad that she wasn't invited to a birthday party, or worried about a boy at school not liking her anymore. Relevant prayer is what challenges us all. My daughters aren't into "seeing the glory of God and his kingdom proclaimed to the ends of the earth," but they do want their best friend to stop lying to them, school to get easier, and their grandmother to walk again. That, my fellow dad, is reality!

No matter how tired you are or how small it feels, start by asking for the equivalent of "daily bread" for your little girl. What is on her heart? School? Friends? Boys? Start where she has an emotional investment. And don't preach while you pray—especially about boys. But after you get the thing rolling, add some big picture stuff, such as your church, missionaries you know, grandparents' health, maybe even the guy she's going to marry one day. Probably the easiest time to do this is at bedtime, but every schedule varies. If you drive her to school, pray on the way (but keep your eyes on the road!). The big thing is to show her the way, and be there with her as she learns to ask her Eternal Father for things you can't provide.

A WORD FROM THE WORD

Some children were brought to Him so that
He might lay His hands on them and pray.
MATTHEW 19:13

Is anyone among you suffering? Then he must pray.
JAMES 5:13

BONUS THOUGHT

I find praying with others the hardest part of my spiritual life. I have no set time for prayer, but I do look for opportunities. It's amazing how dead a set prayer time can feel to your kids and how alive a "let's pray about the thing you just shared with me" can be. Anyone can do it, and I've never had anyone turn me down, not even strangers (which I don't do often). Bringing things to God is humbling, and that's probably why we—especially men—find it tough to do. But isn't that good for me, and for my daughters to see in me?

24. SHOW HER MOTHER RESPECT

(Note to single dads: Do not skip this chapter!)
Before you know it, your daughter will grow into a woman. She will experience romance, and one day probably get married. And you'll be watching to make sure the guy she marries treats her right. . .or else. This is common and good, and gives us dads a sense of paternal righteousness. But as a *husband*, you should take a moment now and then to evaluate something: If you saw some sorry little punk speak to your daughter the way you typically speak to your wife, would you welcome him into the family or drop-kick him all the way to the intensive care unit?

Your little girl is developing her understanding of marriage by watching you interact with your wife. If you constantly undermine your wife or criticize her, your daughter will expect men to treat her that way. It's her version of *normal* because her daddy does it. If, however, you treat your wife with respect by listening to her, complimenting her often, and supporting her endeavors, your girl will expect that same treatment from any guy who tries to get close to her.

Go ahead and set the bar as high as you want for the boys to follow. Treat your wife like you want guys to treat your daughter, and then you can take a righteous delight when your daughter dumps a guy for falling short of the standard you've set.

TAKING INVENTORY

> Do you and your wife argue in front of your kids? Not the spontaneous day-to-day stuff, but the real knock-down, drag-out stuff. If so, this needs to stop ASAP. Go into the bedroom; or, better yet, go to a counselor. And it doesn't matter if you think you're the one in the right.

> Even good marriages develop bad habits. One I have fought more than twenty-five years is my impatient tone when I think an answer is obvious, a comment is dumb, or someone "owes" me something. Have you developed any bad habits of communication toward your wife? A condescending tone? Muttering about her so others can hear? Do you chastise her for things as if she were one of the kids? (You can see I've listed my own failings first. . .so you can add yours now.)

> Divorced Dads: I have never been a single dad, so these are only my thoughts, rather than my experience. Under most circumstances I have witnessed, the kids still want a relationship with both their parents (though I have also seen the occasional exception). Keep in mind that your daughter may be even more sensitive to the way you treat your ex-wife (her mother) than when you were together. Tough? Undoubtedly. Important? Unbelievably.

> Other Single Dads: Again, these thoughts are based on observation, so your experience will have to confirm or modify this. Any good man should be able to treat a woman well. If you are dating, with a daughter who is watching, then the same principles apply as if you were married. Poor communication shows a lack of respect. A girl who sees the most influential man in her life treat a woman disrespectfully will have to wrestle with it the rest of her life.

25. MAKE SURE YOUR WIFE NEVER FEELS IN COMPETITION AS THE QUEEN

To be a princess, a girl needs a dad who's the king and a mom who's the queen. That makes for a great beginning and a really happy ending. Dads who get this mixed up will only create tension that ruins the whole fairy tale. Not to mention it also puts the brakes on activity in the royal bedroom.

Be sure your darling daughter sees you supporting your wife, loving her, and listening to her. A princess who thinks she can get what she wants *over* Queen Mom may soon turn into a little tyrant. And beyond that, you will be teaching her to fail in her own home someday.

THINK ABOUT IT. . .

 As much as you want your little princess to feel special, you cannot afford to let her believe she is more important than your wife. Female competition may run as deep as DNA, but inside your castle, never let it be directed toward your wife. That means not siding with your daughter against your wife, even over small things like bedtime and TV programs. Your wife shares your authority in the house, and the minute your little princess thinks she can divide and conquer is the minute you give up your own crown.

26. GIRLIE GIRLS CAN LEARN TO BE TOUGH, AND TOMBOYS CAN LEARN TO BE TENDER

Femininity has many expressions. After that little bundle wrapped in pink begins to grow up, you may have realized you were blessed with an überprincess—or you may have gotten the *other* blessing: the final installment of the *Terminator* franchise. Some little darlings play happy homemaker, and some pillage the coast, burning down peasant villages. It's all good.

The bad thing would be to allow a stereotype to determine your reaction to the little mystery under your roof. I remember getting jolted out of my "helpless princess" paradigm when my first daughter was four years old. I was working in the yard when she called out, "Daddy! Look!" I turned around to see my dainty baby girl running at me with an enormous toad in each hand. I screamed. She stopped. I vigorously explained that I hated amphibians more than lawyers, and that I wanted both as far away from me as possible. She laughed and ran off to show her older brother. I heard him scream.

We dads need to stretch our kids by challenging them in areas that *seem* to be outside their natural bent. Teach your princess to clean a trout and your swashbuckler to waltz. Both sides are in there, and both sides can be expressed without making your daughter into something she wasn't meant to be.

OUR TRANSLATION

> Each child is a unique piece of God-like pottery, made to be amazing. Force-fitting a child into a mold will be frustrating for both of you. Also, it won't work for long anyway. To be a good dad is to be a student of your daughter, and work out what God made her to be.

BONUS THOUGHT

When I was a kid, my sister, who was a year older, was the tough one. She wanted guns for Christmas and watched war movies with my dad. He and mom never seemed a bit concerned, and gave her the freedom to be herself. She turned out great—she's tall, beautiful, and can shoot. What more could you ask for in a woman?

27. DISCIPLINE HER WHEN SHE NEEDS IT, WITHOUT LETTING HER FLIRT HER WAY OUT

It's a real man who can discipline a pouting daughter. That lower lip is like kryptonite, sucking the strength and willpower out of the most barrel-chested disciplinarian. And the tears! Oh, the tears! Stop, stop, I can't even contemplate the power they wield!

My two girls were Zen masters in their use of these ancient techniques. Often, they would throw their arms around me on the way to the laundry room (our designated spot for a little paddling, which in retrospect has probably contributed to their reluctance to actually do laundry). I was forced to gently pull them away to do what must be done. I could never really spank them, I confess. My son was no problem, since he was a boy, but it was all I could do to give the girls a light tap with a plastic spatula. Being girls, of course, they yelled as if I had cut off their legs. (That made it seem fair to my son, who naturally assumed I had whacked them as good as he got.) I actually got the belt growing up, so no one in my house understands what a good Southern spanking really is. And frankly, I prefer it that way.

No matter how much your resolve is tested by your daughter's wiles, you must be consistent and fair in your discipline. Even if you are a "time outer" and not a spanker, it is unfair in the long run to let your little darling get away with lying, stealing, hitting, or disrespectful behavior. If you are committed to developing her character, you will need to gird yourself for her trickery.

TAKING INVENTORY

> Do you and your wife agree on the method of discipline you use? If there is any divergence on this, it's going to become an unnecessary battleground; so, settle this issue first.

> When it comes to disciplining your kids, do you ever do it in anger? I'm not talking about exasperation, which seems pretty natural to me, but we parents need to be self-controlled during the disciplinary process. We don't help our children when we overreact, or when we let them squirm their way out of accountability.

> Have you set clear standards for your daughter so she knows when and why she will be disciplined? Without clear communication, your discipline will seem arbitrary—and, frankly, you will be more likely to give in when you shouldn't because you're shooting from the hip.

> Do you just say you will discipline, or do you actually do it? Threatening is not disciplining; neither is cutting short what you said would be the consequences. If you say she's lost her phone privileges for twenty-four hours, don't give the phone back after twenty-three. It will tell her she can influence you when you should be influencing her!

28. BE A MR. LEMON FACE

Mr. Lemon Face may not be your thing, but it's easy to do and fun for your girls when they are really young. Scrunch your face as tight as you can (as if you've just sucked on a lemon), then try to talk to and kiss your daughter. That's it. The next time she asks you in church to do Mr. Lemon Face, you'll have a decision to make, now won't you?

TAKING INVENTORY
> Got any silly faces? Use them with your daughter.

29. HIDE NOTES JUST FOR HER

I'm at the age where I don't like surprises, even good ones. But that's just me in midlife. My daughters are a totally different breed. A great way to combine their love of surprises and their love of being remembered is to hide notes just for them.

My daughters started leaving me notes before they could really write. They drew hearts, stick figures of us holding hands, and left kiss-prints with Mommy's lipstick. When they got older and were more literate, the notes told me how much they loved me or how great I was. The girls stuffed them into my briefcase or set them on my pillow when they made the bed. It was such a wonderful feeling for me as a dad. One day, my eldest got really creative and put a note in the coffee jar, knowing I'd be the one to find it, as I am the maker of the sacred nectar every morning. That prompted me to leave a note to her in the sugar bowl. No way a teenager is going to miss that, since even Frosted Flakes aren't frosted enough. That started an exchange that went on for a couple of days.

Get a pad of Post-it notes in bright pink and keep it with you or beside your bed. When you see it, jot down a thought or draw a heart with your daughter's initials in it. Then stick it on her mirror, iPhone, or favorite cereal box. Being surprised by your love requires minimal literacy, and it will be the thrill of her day.

OUR TRANSLATION

> If God has a surprise for us, why not use his methods to delight our little ones? It seems like a great way to imitate him without much theological training.

THINK ABOUT IT. . .

What a small effort this really requires. It costs nothing, and yet makes such an impression. By the way, this is a quick way to move your wife's heart as well.

30. PROTECT HER FROM WHAT SHE FEARS, NOT JUST WHAT YOU FEAR

A sharp stick *will* poke your eye out; if you fall off that fence you *will* break your neck; if you don't floss, your teeth *will* fall out. These are the tip of the parental iceberg of fear. The list goes on to include getting sick, wandering off and getting lost, making the wrong kinds of friends, and not having on clean underwear in case of an accident. I can imagine a hundred bad things that I need to prepare for when it comes to my daughters. That sometimes makes me impatient when they throw in a new fear of their very own creation.

These are ones we dads usually dismiss as "irrational." But in your daughter's mind, *all* fears start as perfectly plausible. There *are* monsters under the bed and in the closet. There *is* an earthquake headed your way like the one on the news. A shark *could* eat her on the second story of a house in the mountains. These fears must be dealt with or nothing else you've planned to do after putting her to bed is going to happen.

My daughters' reality is where I prefer to start. Singing is good; sometimes I shout monsters out from under the bed— the rationale here is that I am scarier than they are. Laughter makes a heart brave.

Security goes to the heart of virtually everything in my little girls' lives. How they see the world and their place in it is affected by whether they feel protected by their parents, and ultimately how well we've transferred that feeling to a real faith in their heavenly Father.

OUR TRANSLATION

> Fear is a wonderful gift, as long as you are fearful (respectful) of the right things. God is too awesome to just slap on the back and call "buddy"—if he weren't awesome and powerful and more than a little intimidating, he wouldn't be much protection for us.

THINK ABOUT IT. . .

No matter how old we get, we can still conjure up new fears. That's why I don't watch the news as much as I used to. When my girls were little, it was almost funny what they came up with to be afraid of, because it was *never* going to happen. As they got older, they feared more sophisicated things that were still unlikely, just not as easy to dismiss. The point is that my opinion of their fears is not as important as helping them face *whatever* it is they're afraid of.

> CAN YOU SAY GAWKY? <

31. TAKE HER TO CHURCH

This one seems pretty obvious. Take your daughter to church.
But for those who don't believe in "organized religion," let
me just say that it is preferable to "disorganized cynicism."
Churches vary in their quality and character, just like any
other organization, just like any individual. Choose one that
is really good, and then try not to muck it up. In other words,
give the church your support and see if that isn't a better
approach than reluctantly going, dragging the family along,
and then complaining later that you "didn't get anything out
of it."

Your little girl will begin—like it or not—to model her
feelings about God from her dad. Notice I did not say she will
be looking at you for her understanding. Just her gut feelings.
So when you set a harsh tone toward church, she will feel
there's no community there, or if there is one, it's not to be
trusted. No pressure here, just the truth.

We all could use a good church (*assembly* if you prefer),
because no one was meant to walk this world alone. Your
little girl is going to have spiritual questions, and she'll have
needs that you and her mom will not be able to address. She
needs to know that she's part of a larger family outside of her
own. Take her to church and help her *become* the church to
someone else. That's being a shepherd of her soul.

THINK ABOUT IT. . .

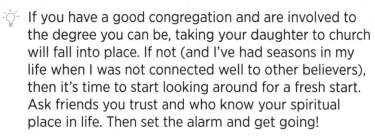 If you have a good congregation and are involved to the degree you can be, taking your daughter to church will fall into place. If not (and I've had seasons in my life when I was not connected well to other believers), then it's time to start looking around for a fresh start. Ask friends you trust and who know your spiritual place in life. Then set the alarm and get going!

32. TEACH HER SUNDAY SCHOOL CLASS. . . AT LEAST ONCE

In my opinion, Sunday school's biggest drawback is that . . . it's on Sunday. That means getting up earlier to go; and, if you're the teacher, it means preparing on Saturday. Well, where's the reward without sacrifice, eh? Nonetheless, you should consider teaching your daughter's Sunday school class at least once, even if you just help the main teacher.

I chose to do it when my daughters were very young, so all I had to do was read Bible stories and do crafts. Arts and crafts give you the chance to use all those skills you learned while building your deck—except that you usually don't get to use a nail gun in Sunday school.

My girls loved the fact that I was with them, and no matter what the dress code was at the church, they were decked out for their class. I have to admit, too, that trying to simplify Bible stories for kids was a great learning experience for me. It may not be your particular strength, but it's worth the effort because it gives your girls a sense of connection to you as a spiritual leader. Just do it when they are about four or five years old so you don't have too much prep time involved. This may also help them to get into a good habit of going to Sunday school when they are older and you are too theologically challenged to lead anymore.

Some dads are actually better at relating to girls when they reach the teen years than when they are kids. If you're one of those guys, plug into your daughter's youth group as a volunteer. (That's another practical idea that we'll save for a later time.)

OUR TRANSLATION

> Try your hand at teaching and experience a part of your heavenly Father you may have never really appreciated.

BONUS THOUGHT

The thought of teaching a children's Sunday school class can be intimidating for some dads. But since most kids' classes come with a prepared text or curriculum, all you really have to do is spend a little time preparing on Saturday night. I taught my youngest daughter's class when she was four years old. It was very basic, to say the least. And we did lots of crafts to take home. I was a huge hit!

33. HOLD HANDS EVERYWHERE

Holding hands is a tender thing, if you think about it. Make a mental list of those you hold hands with. See? The last person I held hands with outside of my wife, daughters, and dear old mom was a tipsy cousin who wanted to dance at a wedding. I mean, the guy just wouldn't let me go!

Kids, both boys and girls, grow up holding hands. It's very natural and comfortable. Then boys realize it's just a control thing and they begin a campaign of resistance. Eventually it degenerates into wrist grabbing and arm yanking and verbal threats—but that's a story for another book. Girls are lifelong hand holders if, and I emphasize *if*, you have done it right as they've grown up. That means it's always been natural. You've offered your hand instead of just grabbing hers. You've let go when *she* decides. You never use it to show off your bear-wrestling grip of steel. Rather, you are gentle and tender and always approachable.

Because hand holding is reserved for a truly small inner circle, it's an opportunity to announce to everyone that this little girl is special. Loved. Secure. Valued. It's a quiet testimony to her, and it's an unmistakable statement to the world around you.

BONUS THOUGHT

Unless you're crossing a busy street with a four-year-old, hand holding is by permission only. Some girls are not going to be interested in holding your big sweaty mitt at any age. But more than likely, the younger your daughter is the more often you'll be allowed to escort her hand-in-hand—so take advantage of it whenever possible. My youngest is now sixteen, and there are still times when she'll reach out and take my hand. It brings back the fondest memories and quietly affirms our mutual delight in each other's company. Heaven!

34. MIND YOUR MANNERS

I was raised in the South, which is to say I learned a few manners. Not that I wanted to, but the consequences for not complying could be brutal. My dad was a true Southerner and a World War II vet, who didn't "cotton" to rude behavior. My mom, a genteel lady, always said that manners would make you stand out in a crowd, especially with girls. She was right.

If you already have a habit of treating women well (and for your wife's sake, I hope you do), then just remember to apply it to your little girl. Your daughter will appreciate your holding the door open for her (like you already do for your wife, right?). It may sound old-fashioned, and I guess it is, but it's also part of showing deference. I still open the car door for my girls unless they bolt ahead to fight for the front seat. (Calling "shotgun!" is frequently ignored at our house by those with swifter feet.)

Anytime you retain the small formalities with your girl (*ladies first* at the church potluck, wiping off the bench for her at the picnic, offering the better seat at a movie, carrying her packages), you say outwardly that you are thinking of her, that she is special because of who she is. It shows that you care. And it sets an awfully high bar for those lousy, ill-mannered boys who will enter her life later. Your daughter will weed out the losers faster because of your manners. And who doesn't want a true prince to woo his little princess?

TAKING INVENTORY

Here is a short list of valuable courtesies that will speak volumes to your daughter:

> Hold the door open for her

> Pull the chair out at special dinners and on dates

> Don't raise your voice to make your point when having a civil discussion

> Offer her the last piece of dessert

> Serve her mom first and then her when carving the turkey, roast, ham, etc.

> Keep eye contact when she's speaking (don't split your attention between her and your phone or the TV)

> Don't interrupt her stories, even if they seem to go on and on

35. HANG HER PICTURES IN YOUR WORKPLACE

My office is a history of my daughters' growth stages. They peer at me from frames with six-year-old eyes, nine-year-old dance costumes, twelve-year-old school shots, sixteen-year-old prom dresses, and eighteen-year-old graduation gowns.

OK, so the girls groan and complain about themselves when they come by to see me, begging me to destroy those embarrassing relics of their development. Sure, they complain that it's a museum of the history of awkwardness and low self-esteem. But deep down they love being the center of attention. They love being displayed for all to marvel at. They love knowing they mean so much to me.

And even if they don't love it all that much, it's my office and my daughters, and I like having them around! So there.

THINK ABOUT IT. . .

 Most workplaces have some flexibility for decorating with family pictures. It might be fun to get one of those multi-window frames and ask your daughter which pictures she would like to put in it. Then she can't blame you for embarrassing her. If your job does not have this flexibility (landscaper, astronaut, waiter), then carry her picture in your wallet and let her know it. Or better yet, load your smartphone up and make her the screen saver. Sure, she'll think you're being ridiculous, but she'll also know you're proud of her.

36. BE PREPARED TO BUY A LOT OF HAIRBRUSHES

Girls are designed by God to be expensive. It keeps guys from thinking they're common. It's not that boys can't be expensive too, but their wants and needs are much easier to understand because they so closely mirror our own (sports equipment, tools, cars, gadgets, fast food, replacing broken stuff). Girls, on the other hand, like things that don't make much sense to us. Decorative things, fancy things, beautiful things, personal things.

My daughters own eight hairbrushes—*each!* Okay, I own eight Philips head screwdrivers, but a screwdriver's *raison d'etre* speaks for itself. What's the difference between one hairbrush and another? How can it possibly matter? Could I even understand it if I were told? Take my advice: Just let some things be.

Almost anything to do with looks, the improvement of looks, the preparation of looks for others, and the like, will be a territory you should avoid if you're looking for a pleasant conversation with a girl or a woman. It's a girl thing and will remain a girl thing no matter how much we might try to argue it down to rational levels. Just buy another hairbrush whenever she asks, and she will think you're smart and wonderful. You'll be out another seven or eight bucks, but ahead on daddy points that you may need to redeem later.

THINK ABOUT IT. . .

 "You are altogether beautiful, my darling." Every girl wants to hear this, first from her mom and dad, and someday from a handsome young man. It's not vanity unless it gets out of hand and her entire identity revolves around her looks. Which is why we dads need to keep our girls focused on internal—and *eternal*—values. But there's nothing wrong with your daughter's natural desire to feel beautiful. Just look at the number of times the Bible includes the word *beautiful* in its description of women (Sarah, Rebekah, Abigail, Tamar, Esther, etc.). Not bad company to be included in.

37. LEARN TO TELL A SQUEAL FROM A SCREAM

The book of Proverbs has a great piece of advice that can be applied directly to our little ones: "Be sure you know the condition of your flocks" (Proverbs 27:23 NIV).

Sheep mostly sound the same to me. But then I've never owned any, much less taken the time to care for one (though I have eaten a few). Thus a *bleat* is a *bleat* is a *bleat*. But with my own "little lambs," I have learned some of their mysterious ways through long exposure and many false alarms. Little girls are *squeally*. That's the only way I can describe it. And sometimes they're *screamy*. A *squeal* is excitement that can no longer be contained. A *scream* is that piercing sound generated by the mere sight of a bug or mouse. Being able to discern between the two is important if you want to avoid racing into a slumber party with a two-by-four in hand, or miss the chance to defend your tender princess from an evil arachnid. It's also essential for those times when you're horsing around, tickle fighting, or boy-teasing. At those times, you'd better know when the squeal of fun begins to fade into a screech of protest.

When your daughter becomes a teenager, the squeal/scream ratio will change to make room for the "screal." This new addition is exactly what it sounds like—an utterance so nuanced in tone that you will go back to square one in trying to tell it apart from the others. One day it will cover fun things, like an unexpected text from a boy she likes or getting asked to be a bridesmaid for the first time; another day it will encompass real horrors—such as breaking a nail right before her big date with the boy who caused the first kind of "screal."

The need to recognize the difference in her reactions is part of "being there" for your girl in the most timely, useful manner. She'll appreciate that you studied her habits in an effort to keep up with her. And it may help you avoid losing your temper at those times when she seems to be "crying wolf," and will ensure that you are her knight in shining armor when she "cries *spider*."

A WORD FROM THE WORD

Know well the condition of your flocks,
And pay attention to your herds.
PROVERBS 27:23

OUR TRANSLATION

> Your job as the dad is to know well the condition of your family. How would a shepherd take care of his sheep if he knew nothing about them? Our families are looking to us to protect them and to provide far more than shelter, food, and clothing; they also need understanding. (And this need continues into adulthood. A husband is exhorted to live in an "understanding way" [1 Peter 3:7] with his wife.)

38. BURY HER HAMSTER/MOUSE/GOLDFISH WITH A DIGNIFIED CEREMONY

Why small pets have such short life spans is a mystery to me—especially when these animals don't do anything. Let's face it, simply being a pet removes an animal entirely from the cycle of evolution. Yep, once you're a pet, life goes from *fittest* to *fattest*. The worst thing they face day to day is being manhandled by a four-year-old. If you've seen *Toy Story 3*, you know what I mean.

Nevertheless, girls want something cuddly or beautiful they can call their own—an early nod to the mothering instinct. So, besides the annoying investment in hamster wheels and forty-gallon aquariums that will end up at next spring's garage sale, we must also prepare for the inevitable heartbreak of death. Let me suggest that you create a plan now so you will not be caught fumbling through the "everything dies someday" talk or become the high priest of a new religion that includes animal salvation.

Choose a burial plot in the yard that's secluded (unless you live on a houseboat, in which case you may have to settle for burial at sea), and have a box in the garage ready to serve as a coffin. Wooden cigar boxes work great for small rodents and such, and they maintain a sense of dignity. You may want to stuff the box with cotton, too, for that extra touch. Don't let your daughter see you dig the hole. It will just be too traumatic—especially if you hit the remains of an earlier pet funeral.

Naturally, the center point of every good pet funeral is the sermon. I used something like this at our first service:

Dear Lord, we are grateful for the short but happy life of Pecan (a pygmy hamster). She was a fine example to us all of living day to day without worry or fear. And thank you that you have allowed us to own pets like Pecan to teach us this important lesson about death, and the design of all things. May Pecan rest in peace. Amen.

If you're lucky, you'll be on your way to the pet store within the hour.

A WORD FROM THE WORD

It is better to go to a house of mourning
Than to go to a house of feasting,
Because that is the end of every man,
And the living takes it to heart.
ECCLESIASTES 7:2

THINK ABOUT IT. . .

- Death is really the most natural *unnatural* thing in the world, since it was never part of God's original plan for his creation. It is his mercy to introduce us to death, as odd as that sounds. He gently allows us (and our kids) to wrestle with our own future through the departure of beloved pets.

39. MAKE THE MOST OF HER INVITATIONS

The time you're able to spend with your daughter is precious. We have no guarantee how many years we'll have our kids under our care, so we must make the most of our opportunities. Every time you say yes to an activity your girl has invited you to participate in, you say yes to the possibility for making a magical memory that neither of you will ever forget.

If I say "Pretty Pretty Princess" to my grown daughters today, it elicits immediate grins and snickers. As little girls, they owned a game by that name. I don't remember who bought it for them, but I do know we made some fond memories playing it. The game consists of an assortment of lovely plastic jewelry—including a 20-carat plastic ring, a colorful bracelet and necklace, two dangling earrings, and the piece de résistance: a royal tiara. The goal of the game was to put on all the pieces of the royal jewelry and thus become the winner.

I can't remember whether another member of the male herd ever walked into the room while I was sporting numerous pieces of jewelry, but I was ready with the definitive response: "Real men play games with their daughters."

For you, it may be sitting down for a cup of tea with the Mad Hatter and your daughter's imaginary friends. Or an invitation to see a chick flick with her. Or a play date with her Barbies and all the accessories. No matter. Just do it.

A WORD FROM THE WORD

Make the most of every opportunity in these evil days.
EPHESIANS 5:16 NLT

*Make the most of every opportunity. Be gracious in your speech.
The goal is to bring out the best in others in a conversation,
not put them down, not cut them out.*
COLOSSIANS 4:5-6 MSG

TAKING INVENTORY

> What are some things that keep you from saying yes to
  your daughter when she asks you to play a game with
  her?

> What is one activity you can make time to do with her
  in the coming week?

> When your little girl becomes an adult and looks back
  on her childhood, what kind of memories do you want
  her to have of you playing games with her?

40. TAKE HER TRICK-OR-TREATING

Some men never grow out of the fun of trick-or-treating. Candy, ninja warriors, Star Wars characters, candy, scary garages, cranking "Monster Mash" for the entire neighborhood to hear, sitting around a fire pit in the driveway, and. . .candy. What's not to like? While our daughters were growing up, it was my job to take Ariel and Belle begging door-to-door while my wife gave out candy on our front porch and warmed the wassail and the pot of chili on the stove in the kitchen.

I knew enough to keep the girls away from the really scary homes where Freddy Krueger and Leatherface lurked behind the bushes, attempting to lure them with candy treats. It was also my job to make sure we hit the homes that served up hot dogs and coffee to all the hungry parents (mostly men) who were in need of a quick pick-me-up as they rounded third and headed for home.

As my daughters can also attest, pumpkin carving—specifically the carving of really cool patterns on Cinderella's carriage—is also predominantly a dad's job. As our girls got older, the patterns we carved, the variety of picks and saws we used, and the time we spent carving them, increased significantly. You should have seen the awesome pirate image—a la Captain Jack Sparrow—I carved, or the Toy Story and superhero pumpkins we've carved the past few years! Every year I must live up to the reputation of carving something bigger and better.

Though some families choose not to celebrate "the devil's holiday," I decided to make "All Hallows' Eve" a significant memory for our girls. The mere mention of it conjures up specific sights, sounds, tastes, and smells—a virtual multisensory experience. Even as they have outgrown the dressing-up years, they still love hanging out with the parentals—bringing friends to share in the carving of the squash, the lighting of the house and yard, and the eating and distribution of sugar.

TAKING INVENTORY

> Besides scary characters on Halloween, what are some other things you need to protect your daughter from?

> What are some ways in which you can use all your daughter's senses to enjoy All Hallows' Eve?

> Just as your heavenly Father delights in you, how can you show your girl that you delight in her?

41. COACH HER TEAM

It's a day my eldest daughter will never forget. One Saturday morning, after a winner's breakfast of donuts and orange juice, we headed to the gym for our first basketball game. My first time coaching a girls team, consisting of third and fourth graders. We had practiced for several weeks. The parents were cheering in the bleachers. Now, armed to the teeth with my white marker board and diagrams of some simple plays, we were ready.

Then the game started, and we quickly found out that the team we were playing from Monfort Heights had been around the gym a bit longer than we had—three years longer to be exact. They knew how to put the ball in the basket, and they did it very proficiently.

After an initial blitz, I called a time-out and started describing to my players what we were going to do to stop the other team's best scorer.

"Girls, look here. We are going to go to a 'box and one' on defense." I told my daughter to guard the other team's scorer, and that everyone else would play a box zone, with two girls at the bottom of the key and two at the top.

When I paused in my presentation, I overheard one of my little point guards ask her friend, "What's a box and one?"

Her teammate responded, "I don't know, but I really think we look cuter in our uniforms than they do!"

I looked at the girls and agreed, "That's right. You guys *do* look so much cuter than the other team! Now, go play ball!"

The blitz continued, though one of our girls eventually scored. . .she made a free throw. The crowd went wild. The final score? 44–1. (Yes, you read that correctly.)

As we got in the car after the game, my wife delivered the crushing blow: "Nice try, dear, but you're not Bob Huggins" (at the time, coach of my hometown University of Cincinnati Bearcats). Ouch. But my daughter will never forget that I coached her!

We moved on to better pursuits, like fast-pitch softball. I spent many days and nights in the backyard teaching my girls how to pitch. The neighbors often heard some yelling. I called it coaching. I saw how much potential both girls had.

A funny thing happened; the madder they got at me while practicing, the harder they threw, and the better they got. Then there was the time when our youngest daughter, after running over the other team's shortstop on her way to third base, cried out for all to hear, "But, Dad, you told me to do that if the girl was in the way!"

Ah, the joy of coaching girls. You may feel that you don't have the know-how, or the patience, or you might rather be coaching boys. But if you will take the plunge and enter into the world of girls sports, and be an active participant as a coach or an assistant, your girls will thank you forever for being involved in this arena of their lives. So many great learning opportunities present themselves that will provide them with life lessons for years to come. However, if your daughter chooses to pursue cheerleading or baton twirling, that's an entirely different story. Try not to throw out your back while attempting to match her jumps.

A WORD FROM THE WORD

My children, listen when your father corrects you.
Pay attention and learn good judgment.
PROVERBS 4:1 NLT

Listen to my instruction and be wise; do not disregard it.
PROVERBS 8:33 NIV

TAKING INVENTORY

> What are some life lessons you learned while participating in sports as a child?

> What is a great piece of "coaching" advice you've received from God that you need to pass on to your daughter?

> What might God be teaching you as you coach girls in sports?

42. ENROLL HER IN AT LEAST ONE MODELING CLASS

Poise and charm are the hallmarks of every princess. And, as dads, you and I will never be able to pass that on to our girls. Ever. Even your wife may have somewhat less authority in this area, because she's "just Mom." My own mother had a very glamorous career in her early years—a model and TV personality, a national pageant winner—but even with that background she was also nurse, cook, disciplinarian, tutor, scrubwoman, and all the other wonderful things a mother is to her family. It took an "expert" from the outside to show my sister how to do certain girl things. My own daughters also seem to respond better to professional instruction, because it transcends the commonplace. (Maybe for the same reason I won't work out at home, but at the gym it's all business.)

Of course, as parents we teach our daughters a lot of the basics, but a girl needs to feel special about her appearance. A modeling class that covers posture, modest makeup techniques, tasteful clothing, healthy eating, etc., can help guide a girl into a very positive self-image without self-absorption. As an outside authority, a good modeling instructor can give a girl confidence to be more elegant and feminine.

There are many modeling agencies that focus on inner beauty and self-esteem first, without pushing girls to conform to worldly standards. Just be careful to keep guiding at home to keep your girl's perspective in balance.

TAKING INVENTORY

> Is there a reputable modeling class available in your area?

> Do they have "personal development" classes for younger girls, that focus on inner beauty and poise?

> If you are in a remote area, or don't find the right kind of classes for your daughter, would you consider connecting with other parents at church or school to offer a worthwhile modeling class based on the elegance and beauty God has placed in all girls?

43. TREAT HER FRIENDS LIKE ADOPTED DAUGHTERS

Girls are natural relationship makers. They always seem to have circles of friends at nearly every stage of life. They are so comfortable with the companionship of their own kind that they actually go the bathroom together when they are out in public. Imagine!

But not all of your princess's friends are treated like royalty at home. Not every dad is the brilliant patriarch you and I are becoming. Not every little girl has a dad who lives at home—or who is engaged in her life, when he is home. What I've learned is that every girl wants someone to tell her she's special. Or, in some cases, to let her know she's not so special that she can't join in the family fun when she's over.

I always try to make my daughters' friends feel as if they are being watched over by a "universal dad." That means I joke with them like my own daughters, make them help clean up just like one of the girls, pay their way to a movie along with my daughters, or chastise them in a fatherly way at 2:00 AM for loud giggling at the sleepover. In fact, if they spend the night, I always pat them on the head or give them a hug and tell them, "That's from your dad." It makes them feel great and makes my own girls feel better about bringing their friends around. And it adds to my vote count for being the coolest dad around.

THINK ABOUT IT. . .

 Though most of my daughters' friends have had great dads, some have not. You and I will never replace that loss in a girl's life, but we can create a safe, fun haven whenever our daughters are hosting them. Nothing is more reassuring to a girl than treating her like family; it tells her she's special. Your own girls will see and appreciate that.

44. AVOID WHAT SHE HATES

My wife stopped hugging her dad at an early age. In fact, she began to avoid physical contact with him entirely. Was he abusive or cold? No. He just thought it was the funniest thing in the world to tickle her whenever she hugged him. Even when she told him how much it bugged her—that she couldn't relax when she got near him—he continued to do it. When he sat down beside her, he'd pinch her knee to see her jump. Although she told him she hated it, it never got through to him that he was driving her away. (I found that out the hard way during our first year of marriage when I pinched her knee.)

You may think you're the funniest guy in the world, but what does your daughter think? Do you drag her out to play the piano in front of guests because you're so proud you can't see it for the torture she thinks it is? Does your daughter dread having you help her with her homework because your impatience makes her feel stupid? Do you insist on dancing with her in front of her friends? (I hope you're not that dense—I had to be told to stop by my wife.)

Maybe you do nothing that annoys her or puts a barrier up between you. But if you're a normal male and she's beginning to become a woman, how long do you think it will be before natural miscommunications start? Pay attention if your princess starts acting as if she wants to be locked away in a tower just to avoid you!

OUR TRANSLATION

> Why cause problems that aren't necessary? It only takes a small amount of effort to identify and change those habits that push your daughter away.

TAKING INVENTORY

> Do you force your daughter to taste weird new food because "it's good for her"?

> Do you sing along with her even though you can't sing?

> Do you wrestle with her too roughly because you think it will toughen her up for the "real world"?

> Do you insist on calling her a pet name she dislikes, even in front of others?

> Do you interrupt her time with friends to do chores she could easily do later, just because you're "the head of the house"?

If you said yes to any of these, you should learn from my mistakes and cut it out.

45. PUT THE TOILET SEAT DOWN

Besides premature baldness and not eating our young, one of the things that separates us men from the lower mammals is civility. Common thoughtfulness. Polite consideration. It's a way of showing others they are important.

When I was in college, one of my mentors from the campus ministry had four daughters. He used to say he was the mascot of a sorority. Whenever he had our men's Bible study over, he insisted we put the toilet seat back down after we used the bathroom. Outnumbered five to one (counting his wife), he had learned to value these kinds of survival skills.

I didn't really pick up the habit until I was married and remembered what he had said: "Let your new wife hit cold water just once in the middle of the night, and you'll see how cold things can really get!"

As my girls grew, they appreciated this simple courtesy, especially after seeing how rare it was at their friends' houses. I started my son on this habit for the sake of his sisters as well as his future wife. You can always tell when a man who is uninitiated in the finer points of porcelain etiquette has been to our house. I often tell those guys, "A princess ought not to have to put down the seat on her own throne."

He who has ears to hear, let him hear.

THINK ABOUT IT. . .

 Putting the seat down is so simple, and so thoughtful, that it's basically a no-brainer. Your wife will appreciate it, your daughters will appreciate it, and it takes almost no real training for you (or for your son). If you have a hard time remembering, do what I did: Write a reminder on the underside of the toilet seat. It will remind you and all the guys who come over, because they are the only ones who will see it!

46. CREATE SURPRISES

Surprises don't have to be elaborate to work their magic. Nothing says "you're special" like being remembered in a way that is unique and personal and totally unexpected. I don't know why flowers work so well on women, but they do almost in proportion to a man's ability to forget that fact. But you can also show your daughter how much she's worth to you without even spending a dime.

Once when my eldest girl and I were coming home exhausted from our jujitsu class (where she typically trained as if she were going into the Octagon), I came to a stop sign and noticed a huge patch of wildflowers. I pulled over into the grass, got out of the car, tore up a big handful of daisies, got back in and presented them to my worn-out little warrior. She was instantly transformed!

Other surprises take time and planning, and maybe some cash. The point is that the surprise should be without a point—for no real reason other than because she's loved. Whether simple or creative, any chance you have to surprise your girl will make her shine.

THINK ABOUT IT. . .

Here's a quick starter list:

- Chocolate works for most girls. But first make sure she's not dieting.

- Unexpected date nights are great.

- Odds and ends from work or travel may mean more to her than you realize.

- Souvenirs from business trips or other times away can be a special treat.

- A silly poem stuck in her lunch box can make her day.

- A handwritten letter mailed to your own house will really get her attention.

- If she has a collection of anything, make a mental note to keep an eye out for those things when you're about your day.

47. ASK HER OPINION, EVEN IF IT DOESN'T MATTER

Let's be honest, most people's opinions don't matter to us, unless it's a doctor, a swing coach, or our boss (and that last one is subject to rigorous departmental debate). We are men, and men can figure out stuff on their own. Just ask our wives.

So what would a *kid* have to tell us? Especially a girl? I don't know, but come to think of it, that seems like a good reason to ask.

With my daughters, I found out that the less I asked their opinion, the less they shared their thoughts. (Duh.) But the more I asked them to chime in, the more they felt free to initiate sharing ideas with me. In the often challenging teenage years, that's worth its weight in gold.

So much of raising a confident, secure daughter rests on the pillars of communication we build as parents—and especially as dads. And it couldn't be simpler than asking your daughter's opinion even when you don't need anyone's opinion.

Asking for input is a way to confirm your daughter's worth to you. Actually taking her advice is way to cement that sense of worth. Start small to keep her safe, then expand to subjects that have some consequence. Start a habit of seeking your little girl's opinion—and incorporating it—and watch her grow in self-confidence, critical thinking, and communication skills. She'll benefit for a lifetime, and one day she'll save her daddy a load of trouble when he thought he already knew all the answers.

THINK ABOUT IT. . .

Here's a simple list to get you going:

- ☼ Does this shirt and tie match? (And all other fashion questions.)

- ☼ What should I get your mother for Christmas?

- ☼ If I were to change jobs, what do you think I'd be good at?

- ☼ Is there anything about our house you'd like to change?

- ☼ Can you give me some feedback on my website?

- ☼ Do you think I was rude to stupid, loud-mouthed Uncle Ned at Thanksgiving?

48. HANG OUT IN THE KITCHEN WITH HER

The kitchen happens to be my favorite room in the house. Yes, I love the solitude (and occasionally great competition) of the basement rec room/movie theater/man cave. And, like any man, I spend my fair share of time in the bathroom. I also love the ambience of my office retreat and work center. But when it comes to spending time with family, nothing can beat the kitchen. And not just because I love to eat (though that really helps sway the vote).

Just as the pumpkin carving with the girls falls to me, so, too, does the dyeing of Easter eggs every spring. For as long as I can remember, on the Saturday evening before the big day, we tune in to Charlton Heston and *The Ten Commandments*, and say all together, "So let it be written, so let it be done." Can't imagine doing anything else on that night.

When the girls were young—before they decided to start sleeping in—Saturday mornings often consisted of my running to the bakery for donuts before they awoke, or whipping up Dad's special blueberry pancake breakfast. I don't know a man who doesn't love breakfast—and Saturdays are especially suitable. Some churches offer men's breakfasts as a means to reach more men. Nothing wrong with that, and I've attended a time or two, but I always preferred staying home on Saturdays and feasting with my girls. And when the occasional Kiwanis fund-raiser or PTA breakfast happened at school, it was a very easy choice to make.

When we sit down at the kitchen table with our daughters, something amazing happens. We find out what they've been thinking about all week. (Maybe not all at once, but if you're patient it comes out.) Whether it's over a bowl of cereal, taco night, strawberry shortcake, a simple meal of grilled cheese formed in the appliance made for just such a thing, or hamburgers and hot dogs slightly charred by me on the grill, table talk gives us great opportunities to see into and speak into our daughters' souls. Thanks to former president Bill Clinton, my wife and I even dared to talk with them about what is considered "sex" in God's eyes. Now, that was an interesting dinner indeed!

A WORD FROM THE WORD

Fix these words of mine in your hearts and minds. . . . Teach them to your children, talking about them when you sit at home and when you walk along the road, when you lie down and when you get up.
DEUTERONOMY 11:18–19 NIV

You know when I sit down or stand up.
You know my thoughts even when I'm far away.
PSALM 139:2 NLT

TAKING INVENTORY

> What's a favorite dish of your daughter's that you could plan to fix for her all by yourself?

> Each time you sit down at the kitchen table with your daughter, think of one or two good questions you can ask to get her talking, perhaps something like this: "What was the best thing that happened at school this past week?" or "If you could be any superhero, who would it be and why?"

> What are some topics that could best be discussed with your daughter at the kitchen table?

49. PLAN A SPECIAL TRIP FOR HER

MVP quarterback Phil Simms of the New York Giants was the first to broadcast, "I'm going to Disney World" after winning Super Bowl XXI on January 25, 1987. With the exception of 2005, every year since, a player from the winning team in the Super Bowl has exclaimed this phrase or its counterpart, "I'm going to Disneyland." Why? Beside the fact they are paid to say it, and they get a free trip out of the deal, the answer is simple. They are smart men.

There are some reasons you might offer as excuses for not going to visit the Mouse and all his friends: it's too crowded; it's too expensive; you don't want to get run over by strollers; you don't want to hear "buy this and buy that" constantly; the money could be used instead for world missions or hurricane and earthquake relief; you don't want to feel like a foreigner in your own country. Decent points, all. I've said a few of them myself. But I'd offer the following points to build a case for taking your daughter to Walt Disney World:

> Your family will love you.

> With some well-thought-out advance planning, you'll make a ton of memories.

> Everybody loves a parade (and Disney knows how to do parades).

> You'll give your daughter a tour around the world without having to leave America.

> Disney has the best customer service anywhere.

> You can eat breakfast with the princesses in the castle.

> You'll eat like a king (again, with advance planning).

> You'll see the coolest pyrotechnics known to man.

> Your daughter will never forget it.

The first time we went to WDW, we awoke our daughters from their slumber very early in the morning and told them we had a big surprise for them—but didn't tell them what it was. As we got close enough to the Magic Kingdom for our oldest daughter to figure out the surprise destination, she exclaimed, "It's my dream come true." We've been going ever since.

If going to a Disney park doesn't fit your budget or interests, why not think about some other kind of special trip. . .such as an overnighter in a nearby city, a camping trip, or a two-day adventure at a water park or amusement park?

A WORD FROM THE WORD

I concluded there is nothing better than to be happy and enjoy ourselves as long as we can.
ECCLESIASTES 3:12 NLT

TAKING INVENTORY

> To many people, Disney World is known as the "happiest place on earth." Why do you think this is so?

> If the Magic Kingdom is the happiest place on earth, what will God's eternal kingdom, heaven, be like?

> This coming week, how can you give your daughter a glimpse of the true happiness that is God's kingdom?

5O. BE PETER PAN

At first glance, this is one your wife may not appreciate, but your daughters definitely will. Here's the lesson: Don't grow up. Has your wife ever accused you of that? Yeah, mine too . . .numerous times. Too many men never grow up—in a bad sense. I'm not encouraging the kind of childish behavior that is selfish, causing a man to seek only his own pursuits, to shirk responsibilities, to go to Vegas on a gambling binge by himself, to spend all his time playing video games or golf, and act as if he's a whiny professional athlete who thinks everyone else should just put up with his antics—and deal with it. I'm not suggesting you be a slacker.

I'm talking about the kind of childlike innocence that Jesus affirmed (see Matthew 18:3–4). We should never grow old in the sense of losing the wonder and curiosity that characterizes preschool children. One of my favorite movies is *Hook*, in which Robin Williams plays Peter Banning, the man who once was Peter Pan. When the movie opens, he's a dad who is more concerned about making business deals on his cell phone than making it on time for his son's baseball game. And there's a huge price to pay for his misaligned priorities. Peter spends the rest of the movie trying to get his kids back!

In a poignant moment, in which his wife is trying to arrest Peter's attention (and mine, too), she delivers the line, "They grow up so fast."

If you're a father of a two- or three- or thirteen-year-old, you might not agree at this very moment. But trust me on this. It's true. Much has been written about how kids today are losing their innocence at much younger ages. They are hitting puberty earlier, being asked to grow up in ways they should not have to, and having to care for younger siblings due to family dysfunction. Please, as far as you can control, don't force your daughter to grow up too soon. Participate in the wonder of play with her. Unless. . .you become like little children. . .

TAKING INVENTORY

> Depending on the age of your daughter, what would it mean for you to "get down on her level"?

> What is something so childlike and innocent your daughter would never expect you to do? Go for it.

> In what area of your spiritual walk is God telling you to slow down and enjoy the rhythm of a child?

51. TEACH HER TO LOSE GRACIOUSLY

I have a friend I used to play tennis with. Before a match, we'd say to each other, "Winning is good, but sometimes it just builds your ego. But losing can help build your character." It helped take away some of the sting of defeat when I lost. I distinctly remember, however, saying to him after he had won several days in a row, "I've got enough character in my life right now. It's your turn. I'm going to kick your butt."

Building character is good, as is building confidence in your ability to do things well. Your daughter needs to learn how to do both. As she grows up, don't be afraid to beat her at H-O-R-S-E in your driveway, or in chess, badminton, or speed croquet. A time or two, my wife heard one of my daughters moaning about it not being any fair while I was beating her at something in the backyard. My wife would yell from the kitchen window, "What's going on out there?" And, my reply would simply be, "I'm helping her with some character building. It's my job."

As she grows older, it's important that your daughter have some experience in this area, as she'll find out in school and in the real world that we can't always win. Teaching her how to correctly count, and take her turn, and follow the rules, are all part of it. If she's still young, however, you'll need to be very selective in the character-building department. She should win most of the time you play her in anything. At what point it's okay to start beating her is tough to say. It probably varies from kid to kid. I can remember throwing a few Candy Land games. I don't think I ever beat either of my girls in that one. If you want to play a game in which nobody wins, choose Monopoly.

Endurance develops strength of character,
and character strengthens our confident hope of salvation.
ROMANS 5:4 NLT

Don't lose a minute in building on what you've been given,
complementing your basic faith with good character,
spiritual understanding, alert discipline, passionate patience,
reverent wonder, warm friendliness, and generous love,
each dimension fitting into and developing the others.
2 PETER 1:5–7 MSG

TAKING INVENTORY

> What are the godly traits you'd like to see your daughter develop in her character? Make a list.

> What specific plans can you put in place to help her develop those traits?

> When's the last time your daughter beat you in a game? How did you help her learn to win graciously?

52. MAKE HER PURSUITS YOUR PURSUITS

One of the tasks of parenting our kids is to raise each one in the way that is best for that child, according to his or her unique wiring. Proverbs 22:6 challenges us, "Start children off on the way they should go, and even when they are old they will not turn from it" (NIV). That phrase, "the way they should go" could be translated "according to their own bent." An old English proverb says, "As the twig is bent, so grows the tree."

One of the temptations we all face is to raise our kids according to what *we* think they should be, not necessarily what God has created them to be as evidenced by their own bent, talents, and individual DNA. No doubt you've seen men who try to live vicariously through their kids. Perhaps they didn't achieve as much as an athlete as they'd hoped, so they do everything possible to make that happen for their kids. Maybe they wish they hadn't stopped taking piano lessons as a child, so they're determined not to let their kids bow out. This may even happen subconsciously. You need to be alert to the possibility that you could do this to your daughter unknowingly.

One way to prevent this from happening is to make your daughter's pursuits *your* pursuits. This may be a real challenge if you are athletic and she's not—or vice versa. I know a family in which the father was a high school football coach, but his son was more interested in being the drum major and marching with the band than he was in throwing the football with his dad. His two daughters, on the other hand, got the athletic genes passed on to them.

If you are more of a *feeler* than a *thinker*, you will probably get this intuitively; but if you are less of a feeler, you will need to work at it. Dig deep to see why your daughter is pursuing the things she is, and be willing to engage with her to show her that you care about the things she is invested in.

If you will raise her according to her bent, it will pay off in big dividends later. That's not a guarantee, because we all (including your daughter) enjoy something called free will—but it's a very strong possibility.

A WORD FROM THE WORD

Work willingly at whatever you do, as though you were working for the Lord rather than for people.
Colossians 3:23 NLT

Be thankful in all circumstances, for this is God's will for you who belong to Christ Jesus.
1 Thessalonians 5:18 NLT

TAKING INVENTORY

> What words would you use to describe your daughter's bent?

> What do you know about her specific personality profile? How does it mesh with yours? What are the strengths and weaknesses of your relationship at this point?

> In what ways can you be "all in" in a greater way with her specific pursuits?

53. BUY HER CHOCOLATE

Did you know that 15 percent of women in America send *themselves* flowers on Valentine's Day? That's a travesty. Your wife may be at the stage in life where she says she doesn't want flowers and candy—there are more practical things she'd rather have than flowers, and the candy would use up her total allotment of Weight Watchers points for a week. Now, if Lean Cuisine ever came out with a lo-cal frozen chocolate treat in the shape of a heart, I'd be very interested!

Through the years, my wife bought our girls books, DVDs, pajama pants with cute hearts on them, and gift cards. My assignment was always the same: cards and chocolate. Hallmark has more than 1,330 different cards specifically for Valentine's Day—so you should be able to find something suitable. When I've exhausted the decent cards for young adult women, I revert to the sparkly princess cards designed for little girls. Bonus points for a Disney theme. They're still a winner! And in case you don't already know this, always buy chocolate you would enjoy eating yourself. You may inherit the pieces your daughter doesn't want. And what if she gets sick during February and you don't want the good stuff to spoil? You must be prepared to man up for this kind of thing.

Chocolate is good. It might even be considered one of the four food groups. Make your daughter feel special by reminding her that her heavenly Father created chocolate for her. The fact is, your daughter needs chocolate. . .from you. The day may come when you are not the only one buying your daughter cards and gifts for Valentine's Day. But until then, buy her chocolate.

A WORD FROM THE WORD

*If you sinful people know how to give good gifts
to your children, how much more will your heavenly
Father give good gifts to those who ask him.*
MATTHEW 7:11 NLT

TAKING INVENTORY

> How have you done in the gift-giving department with your daughter? Is it something you struggle with or are you great at it?

> How can you exhibit God's love to your daughter in a greater way this week?

> Besides giving her chocolate on Valentine's Day, what other creative things could you do to show her your love?

54. MAKE THE MOST OF WHATEVER YOU DO

When my girls were little, they looked forward to putting on their swimsuits and washing the cars with me on a Saturday or Sunday afternoon. OK, maybe washing the cars was not their first priority. Maybe they were more looking forward to getting sprayed with the hose—and spraying their dad. Or maybe they just liked spending time *with me.*

I have a good friend who told me she looked forward to doing whatever her dad was doing—just to be with him. He worked long hours and traveled some, so she seized the opportunities to participate in whatever he did during his spare time. That might mean watching him change the oil in the car, or sitting on the counter while he shaved, or being carried piggyback to breakfast. But whatever it was, she knew she needed to enjoy the time with him while she had it.

Later in life, when she lived in a different city, she was known to hold up her phone to her "sick" car, and ask her dad to diagnose the problem over the phone. Now, that's a talent many men don't have! When her dad died a few years ago, I was honored to officiate at his graveside service. He was a man who was very thoughtful of others, always seeking to make them feel important. In the weeks and months before his death, he had sent heartfelt notes to loved ones and friends, thanking them for what they had meant to him. At the cemetery, I shared some of the words he had written to my wife and me. What a powerful legacy he left.

We don't know how much time we'll have with our daughters, so make the most of the time you have—while you still have it.

TAKING INVENTORY

> What are some everyday activities you do that you could invite your daughter into?

> If you work long hours or have to travel as part of your job, what are some ways you can make the most of the time you have with your daughter?

> When's the last time you wrote a handwritten note and left it in your daughter's room. . .just because?

55. SCHEDULE A DATE NIGHT

I expected dating to end when I got engaged. I figured after that we'd just "be together." But I swiftly learned, as all men do, that I must continue to "date" my fiancée and—shockingly—even my wife! I was soon introduced to a concept called "married dating," which essentially means giving up night after night of ESPN to get out of the house and give my wife my undivided attention. It seems to be a hardwired belief in women that they are to be treated special. Go figure.

This need for attention and escape from the routine starts out very early in our daughters. Getting our time and attention is their blessing. Again, go figure. So here are the basic parameters for a successful event, with or without a budget.

Don't throw it together at the last minute. Even little girls will figure it out if you do. They all like to think you were thinking about them. Your daughter is a princess, and as such deserves the royal treatment. I guess I should also mention that you should plan stuff *she* likes. That hasn't always occurred to me, so I'm putting it in print. My daughters don't want to eat steak in front of the TV, or grab a hot dog on the way to a mixed martial arts tournament. Maybe yours do, but mine want a *dining experience* and a trip to Barnes & Noble. Fortunately, I am cultured enough to enjoy that too, and they have *Guns & Ammo* magazine there anyway. I've had to learn some of this by trial and error. Planning ahead will give your daughter the feeling of being important, and having a plan B will rescue you if you get it wrong. Most of my plan Bs involved the mall. The mall, in this case, covers a multitude of sins.

THINK ABOUT IT. . .

- ⌁ Who is the best person to set your daughter's expectations for how she should be treated? The last person you want doing that is the first boy she likes. Your date nights are more than just fun, more than just time to get to know her—as valuable as that is. It sets her earliest expectations of how she should be treated by a member of the male species. Her standards will be higher (and safer) when the boys start coming around because her dad held the door for her, listened to her without interruption, spoke gently, and made her feel secure and free. Set the bar high when she's young, and she'll more likely be discerning later on.

TAKING INVENTORY

> What is your daughter's favorite restaurant?

> What kinds of things does she like to do when she dresses up?

> Are there any places she's been talking about that you could make into a surprise date?

> Does your wife have any insights for you? (She has probably heard a few ideas during those late night talks that dads don't get.)

56. TEACH HER TO STAND UP STRAIGHT

Body language communicates, whether we intend to send a message or not. I see beautiful girls everywhere slumped over like it's just too much trouble to use their spines. My dad harped on it all the time with us—especially with my sister. She was a tall girl and tended to feel as if it were a hindrance. Being a military veteran, my father always told her: "Shoulders back, chest out, straighten up, and look people in the eye." Not that I would include "chest out" in instructing my own daughters today, but the point was made.

Nowadays, it seems as if slumping teenage girl syndrome has reached epidemic proportions. Next time you're at the mall, count the number of girls who seem to be burdened by an invisible backpack. Fully outfitted Sherpas on Everest stand up straighter than that. What's weighing them down? My guess is a real lack of self-confidence and proper male attention. As your little girl develops into a somewhat bigger girl, she needs more attention, rather than less, from her dad. Sure, she's gaining more independence, but her need for affirmation from you is at a critical point. She is either going to hide her development and feel awkward, or understand it and embrace it. If you teach her as a child to stand up straight and look people in the eye, it will be easier for her to do it as she grows taller and. . .more womanly. Don't worry, if the confidence she exudes doesn't counterbalance the new male attention, you can always lock her in her room until she slumps from old age.

Is this just me, because of the influence of my father? Doesn't confidence show in a person's body language? And you don't have to be an extrovert to be confident, either. If your daughter is naturally shy, that doesn't mean she can't be confident in herself. Teaching my daughters to stand up straight was fairly easy. Frankly, they inherited most of their self-confidence from their mother—or, as I like to call her, "She who cannot be stopped."

However you do it (and by that I mean with genuine ongoing affirmation), get your girl to stand up and look the world in the eye. It will make a difference in the kinds of boys she attracts, the kind of job she lands, and the way she is treated for the rest of her life. Let the *slumpers* be someone else's kids!

57. PROTECT HER PRIVACY, INCLUDING DIARIES AND PHONE CALLS

Nothing spells the end of trust like an invasion of privacy. You know how it feels when someone picks up your financial folder, logs on to your computer, or listens at the door when you're on the phone. And it doesn't help if the intrusion was entirely accidental—it still hits below the belt. Our little girls are designed to require more privacy than boys. The Lord made females to be somewhat mysterious to keep males interested. Their need for privacy surfaces very early on. They may not want you to see what they are planning to wear, or they may want mom to help them do something you used to be quite adequate for, or it may be that they are becoming aware of their changing physical features. Perhaps they're just delighted by the fact that they can have secrets to write in a diary. *Feeling* sneaky is fun; it's *being* sneaky that's bad.

God gave us dumb people to learn from: I knew a man who thought that, just because it was "his house," he didn't have to knock before going into his kids' rooms, even after his daughters were teenagers. Needless to say, he destroyed all sense of trust with his girls. Don't feel put off when your daughter starts to want more privacy, because it's a sign she's growing up. Of course, privacy ends at destructive things like smoking, drinking, drugs, or sex. And you need to be sure to warn her about the dangers of sharing private information on the Internet. But long before those become a possibility, your little one will be writing in a diary and texting friends about boys in her class. Respect that little display of independence and it will develop trust that will serve you well if the dangerous stuff starts to rear its ugly head.

A WORD FROM THE WORD

He who is faithful in a very little
thing is faithful also in much.
Luke 16:10

OUR TRANSLATION

> It's a very small thing to grant your daughter privacy. But the payoff is huge.

THINK ABOUT IT. . .

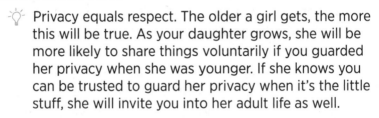 Privacy equals respect. The older a girl gets, the more this will be true. As your daughter grows, she will be more likely to share things voluntarily if you guarded her privacy when she was younger. If she knows you can be trusted to guard her privacy when it's the little stuff, she will invite you into her adult life as well.

58. MAKE UP CODE WORDS

Crazy as it seems, you and I are not as cool to the next generation as we were to our peers. In fact, we may be outright nerdy and begin to create noticeable social tension just about the time our daughters reach puberty. It's very odd timing.

Your daughter will begin stretching her little wings of independence more aggressively as she starts developing and is surrounded by others of her own annoying pre-teen kind. Biochemically speaking, her assertion that you are "gross" and "creeping her out" is natural. These and other self-conscious pejoratives are merely expressions of her brain being rewired to cope with boys, the changing of her body, and general adulthood. Regardless, she will still need guidance and discipline to make it through this phase without being put up for adoption. Thankfully, there is an easy way around this communication conundrum: secret code words.

Secret code words allow you to tell her something in front of her friends without embarrassing her. For example, she needs to start using deodorant, but forgot right before she heads out the door to spend the night. You call her *schmellobum* and she knows to run back and take care of things without anyone else knowing she stinks. Or she's not done with her homework or chores and has friends drop by to waste her time. You tell her, "It's okay, *Martha Stewart*," which of course means that she may indulge now, but will pay for it in housework later. Or a sketchy guy you've never met pops up at the front door to see her, and you decide to let her know you will *open the whole can*, if necessary. I've no doubt you can figure out what that means.

TAKING INVENTORY

> What code words have you already established with your daughter?

> Are there any awkward topics that could really use a good code word for both of your sakes?

> Does your wife cringe at anything you call by its technical name? (Please don't defend medical terms for things if your wife doesn't agree, even if you're a doctor.)

59. ENCOURAGE INSIDE JOKES

Nothing seems to say "inner circle" among people more than sharing a private joke or two. Your princess wants a unique relationship with you, even if you have ten other daughters. One great way to indicate this is to have private jokes. They reference pleasant past memories and give you both a sense of fun while confirming a unique closeness. You can sometimes agree to let others in on the joke too. It makes for a special club.

Real-life experiences make the best inside jokes. When my first daughter was about two and a half, we were leaving my mother's house and I reached for her hand to walk her down the front steps. She pulled back, so I reached again. She stuck her little face out and announced in firm, measured words, "I BY MY SELF." Then she proceeded to walk down without my assistance. That has become our inside joke (which I got permission to share with you here) whenever she asserts her independence—in a positive way, of course.

THINK ABOUT IT...

 Finding humor in everyday events comes naturally in most families, I know; but look for opportunities to grab a moment and make it an inside joke. They grow in meaning over time. They communicate volumes in a few words.

60. NEVER FRIGHTEN HER!

I know you're hilarious. You're "The Man" when it comes to practical jokes and crazy stunts. Like a lot of guys, you think you're the life of the party. So let's just keep it that way. Don't try to share this special gift with your little princess. You will just come across as a scary, dull-witted, disturbing moron.

Our daughters need to be able to trust us. Hiding behind the door or under the bed is *not* the way to do that. Fear is not the way to a little girl's heart. Appalling, I know, but save your wild and crazy gags for the next guy's night out, lodge meeting, or thirtieth, fortieth, or fiftieth birthday party. (After about fifty, though, this is no longer a good idea.)

If it takes more explanation than this, you should see a psychiatrist.

A WORD FROM THE WORD

*Fathers, do not exasperate your children,
so that they will not lose heart.*
COLOSSIANS 3:21

TAKING INVENTORY

> Do you like to hide and scare your daughter? Sons? Wife?

> Cut it out.

61. DON'T MAKE PROMISES WITHOUT QUALIFIERS

Promise Keepers has been an excellent movement among Christian men for more than twenty years now. But even before they came along, every man belonged to—like it or not—Promise Makers. Easy to make 'em, hard to keep 'em. And, for some reason, it's easiest of all to excuse ourselves from our promises, because of. . .of. . .stuff that came up.

Basically, our little girls are braver than we are. They take us at our word, but we don't believe anything we hear and only half of what we see. They expect us to follow through on everything that even halfway hints at a promise. In fact, they will assume we mean what we say, period. How gullible, right?

Of course you and I *want* to be able to follow through, it's just that sometimes things really do get wild and wooly. So why not just tell your daughter the facts of life on predicting the future: It's not entirely possible. She will be better off if you are honest, and not as disappointed if things work against you—things like a last-minute crisis at work, a flat tire, or a migraine. Tell her that "Lord willing" you'll be at her recital; that unless your plane is late, you'll make her birthday party; that unless you and Mommy get a chance to go out for a long overdue date night, you'll watch a movie with her. She'd rather hear it straight, and you'd rather not have to sound like you're making excuses when something unforeseen really does come up. Sometimes you just can't control your circumstances. So, be honest about it, and you'll sleep better.

THINK ABOUT IT. . .

- What realities do you face everyday that could interrupt your best intentions? Do you travel? Are you a firefighter? Do the letters MD appear on your business card? These are things that should be factored in gently when you make a promise.

- Do you ever make promises to your daughter before you've discussed it with your wife? Ponies, Disney World, various body piercings—it's best to wait on issues that need your wife's input, or the result may be a good guy/bad guy scenario. You do not ever want to make your kids peg one of you as "the fun one." Bad idea. Bad.

62. NOTICE THINGS LIKE HER HAIR, HER CLOTHES, HER SHOES, HER TALENT

If beauty is in the eye of the beholder, then being noticed is in the mind of the beheld. Some people don't want to be noticed at all—spies, adulterers, criminals—and that provides the basis for the security camera industry. Some people avoid attention because they are insecure and don't believe any good opinion is being formed of them. Your daughter wants attention, and you—whether you deserve it or not—are at the top of the list of preferred audiences. Of course, her mom's opinion matters too, but ultimately your wife is one of *them*—a girl. You, on the other hand, are one of *those*. And that counts for a lot.

You may not be Sherlock Holmes, with keen powers of observation, but it doesn't take much to learn to notice an eager little princess. Make it a habit to pause to look at her. If something has changed, mention it. Compliment little things, such as how she's wearing her hair that day, or the color she's wearing that looks good on her. When she wants to sing you a song or dance you a dance, take the time to enjoy it. Then do something she might not expect: Give her specific feedback and praise. When all you say over and over is, *"Wow, that was great,"* all she hears is, *Dad's not paying attention*. But when you notice details, and mention them, she knows she's the center of attention. A very nice place for you to put her.

OUR TRANSLATION

> Healing and growth reside in our words. And our daughters are listening to everything we say about them. It's wise to consider our words from their perspective first.

TAKING INVENTORY

> If you're like me and leave for work before your daughters get dressed, your first opportunity to comment on things will probably come in the evening—when, like most dads, you're tired and not thinking about such things. When do you first see your daughter all dressed up and ready to face the world? Plan for that moment. Be ready with some specific praise and affirmation.

> Can you, right now, accurately describe your daughter's hairstyle? Would you be able to tell if she got something done to it while you were at work?

> I know that when girls get older, clothes come into the house like water and electricity—24/7. So, noticing something new may be tough—it's all new. But what about something that really looks great? Would it occur to you to say something? Staying in tune with opportunities is the key.

63. BE SWIFT TO APOLOGIZE WHEN YOU HURT HER FEELINGS, EVEN IF YOU DON'T UNDERSTAND WHY

It's a law of the universe that men don't fully comprehend women, starting with our little baby girls. They are made to be more sensitive and intuitive and tender than boys. That alone makes them virtual foreigners in our homes. It also puts an enormous obstacle in the way of our being our normal brutish, manly selves. But that's the way it is, and no matter how much we think we *"didn't do anything!"* we will from time to time trounce our daughters' feelings.

The more you defend yourself during these times, the more the women and girls in your life will gang up on you—and no rational man will come to your aid, for fear of being associated with you. It's during that one fleeting moment of sanity before you get bent out of shape for being accused of emotional thuggery, that you can redeem the whole situation. Man up and apologize. And I mean apologize for what your little girl thinks you did that hurt her feelings. Most likely, you won't understand it. But this is not the time to pour on an analytical assessment and try to talk her out of her feelings. (In fact, there's never a good time for that.) It's not possible, because her feelings are already hurt, and trying to convince her that they're not is a great big way of saying, "You're dumb for feeling that way." And don't linger; it just makes it worse for both of you (and allows your wife time to reload).

Do this then, my son, and deliver yourself;
Since you have come into the hand of your neighbor,
Go, humble yourself, and importune your neighbor.

PROVERBS 6:3

OUR TRANSLATION

> Don't allow your relationship with your daughter be taken captive by your pride. Apologizing is the key to reconciliation and restoration.

THINK ABOUT IT. . .

Apologizing for your mistakes is just plain mature, whether it's with your daughter or anyone else. But with your daughter in particular, it's a powerful healing tool.

Here's an important point: Do not ask for forgiveness. That just puts pressure on her. She will forgive you when she's ready; your job is to humble yourself and say you're sorry.

64. GO ON A MICRO DATE

The idea of going on a date with your girl may be tough when you're busy. But the pressures and priorities on your schedule are completely lost on her. She's under the impression you *want* to spend time with her. (Crazy, huh?) And when you don't spend time with her, she thinks there's something wrong with *her*. I empathize with other busy-stressed-overworked dads on this one, but it doesn't make us any less responsible for spending time with our girls.

In the in-between times, when a real outing is impossible, I take my girls on "micro dates." It's sort of like snacking between meals, but in a good way.

The keys to a micro date are *spontaneity* and *simplicity*: Walk around the block with your girl, ride bikes up and down the street—anything that will put the two of you together for a few meaningful minutes and can be done on the spur of the moment. Look for times that are naturally slow, like just before dinner, or just after. It can be as simple as taking her along on an errand on Saturday and swinging through the drive-thru for a frosty. It could be reading on the back porch for a few minutes before you head out on a business trip. Heck, it could even be taking her with you to fix your mother's dripping faucet, as long as you make her the center of it all. Micro dates may not replace more significant times together, but they will definitely make those spontaneous times together more meaningful.

A WORD FROM THE WORD

Jesus called for them, saying, "Permit the children to come to Me, and do not hinder them, for the kingdom of God belongs to such as these."
LUKE 18:16

OUR TRANSLATION

> If you think your schedule has too many demands, consider Jesus' schedule. No excuses. Look for opportunities. They are part of your everyday life.

65. GIVE HER A THOUGHTFUL PRESENT, JUST FROM YOU TO HER, ON SPECIAL OCCASIONS

Special occasions for women are serious events, whereas a man can see any number of things as a special occasion: the grand opening of a new pub, every home game, an unexpected invitation to play golf, a rainy Saturday that keeps the lawn mower safely in the garage.

I think testosterone may block our understanding of the finer things in life, like relationships. Girls are preset to over-expect things on their birthdays, Valentine's Day, Christmas—and don't even get started on "anniversaries," which can be any event they think we should remember. My suggestion is to take advantage of this bent and knock one out of the park by giving your daughter a present just from you. It's cool to share a big item, such as a bike or a pony, with your wife or even the whole family. But the little things make the biggest difference. A pair of earrings, a bracelet, a leather journal—anything personal from you will tell your girl that she's remembered and loved. And it doesn't even have to cost that much. . .it's being your special girl that's priceless.

THINK ABOUT IT. . .

- If your daughter is special (which she is), treat her that way. If all else fails, flowers really do work. And you can get them everywhere. When my daughters were younger, I used to keep small tokens in my drawer so I didn't have to go out and get something if I forgot. Those tokens later turned into gift cards to their favorite stores. Here are some special events you may not recognize:

- First day of school

- Last day of school

- First day of a new job

- The day she is leaving for camp

- The day you come back from a long trip

- Driver's license day

66. TAKE HER WITH YOU TO TELL THE BARBER HOW HE SHOULD CUT YOUR HAIR

So you *say* you trust her opinion? You *say* she has good taste? Well, let's just lay it on the line. Too many of us dads aren't aging very well anyway. And most of us have less hair to work with these days. The next time you get a haircut, let your daughter go with you. Even if you can't bring yourself to let her pick out a blue Mohawk, you can at least let her give her approval of the final results.

Long ago, I began shaving my head, but I still get my daughters' opinion. Not only do they approve of it (thanks to Bruce Willis for showing us the way more than a decade ago), they often reprimand me for letting the fringe get *too long*! A few years ago, we were having a cookout with about twenty friends, one a single dad with his fourteen-year-old daughter. As we were talking about middle-age stuff, I looked at this guy and challenged him to let me shave his head right on the spot. (He still had that Mr. Burns ring of thick hair—the kind that says, "I don't own a mirror."). As he tried to change the subject, I asked his daughter what she thought. She got very animated; and to his credit, he took her advice. The results were a great improvement and she was so pleased to be the one, out of all of us, who convinced him. Incidentally, she helped him update his wardrobe too, and now he's happily remarried. (Your individual results may vary, please consult your own daughter before getting excited.)

TAKING INVENTORY

> Have you ever allowed anyone else to make the final decision about your hairstyle? (I mean since your mom stopped trimming it in the middle of the kitchen with a bowl?)

> What would stop you from letting your daughter decide what you should look like?

> How bad can it get? You're probably not as cool looking as you think anyway.

6**7**. TEACH HER YOUR FAMILY HERITAGE

Sometimes, girls get the short end of their family history because it's assumed they will marry and change their names anyway. The son "carries on the family name." I grew up surrounded by family history and Scottish heritage, even though we were a good three hundred years removed from our ancestors' arrival in the New World. Ironically, though I was the "name bearer," it was my sister who had the real interest in our family tree. She's the one you go to on my side to find out who's who.

I'd like my daughters to know where they came from, just as any princess would. Royals take great pride in their lineage and it gives them a sense of belonging and identity. Likewise, this knowledge creates security in our own little princesses and may lend to their future sense of purpose. Genealogy might be something you've never even thought of, or it may be difficult to trace your ancestry very far. But there's always you and your wife! For your kids, that's a generation worth remembering. Tell your princess about your life and background, and what you know about your parents and grandparents.

If you're lucky, your daughter may have a grandparent or aunt or uncle who's really into ancestry.com. If that's the case, your work will be mostly done. For a kid, that's a lot of history right there. And if you can't trace your lineage all the way back to Noah, so what? Share with your girl everything you know and she'll have a better sense of who she is.

A WORD FROM THE WORD

I bow my knees before the Father, from whom every
family in heaven and on earth derives its name.
EPHESIANS 3:14–15

OUR TRANSLATION

> Family is God's plan for mankind. No culture has ever developed without the family as its basic unit, whatever that unit may have looked like throughout history. The entire story of Israel in the Old Testament is built on families, clans, and tribes. And in some spiritual way, God the Father is connected to every family; the Father intends that we all be connected to his family.

68. PHYSICAL AFFECTION HAS NO SUBSTITUTE

Girls love—I mean really *thrive* on—physical affection. God wired them for caressing, kissing, cuddling. Most likely, your daughter won't have a problem with getting her back scratched, her head rubbed, or her shoulders squeezed. Do you think day spas discovered this by accident? Physical affection is the surest way to instill a sense of feminine identity in a girl. This is God's gift to a dad: expressing the purest form of masculine love—a love that does not demand anything in return.

Some of us dads aren't comfortable with being gentle and affectionate. Perhaps we watched too much John Wayne or Dirty Harry growing up. But for your daughter's sake, you can learn. For example, pulling her close is not an opportunity to poke her in the ribs, squeeze her knee, or tickle her until she would kill you with a pencil if she had one—that's your dumb sense of humor; she's not laughing. Rough or insensitive touch teaches her to keep her distance because she can't trust you. Instead, stroke her arm or pat her head. (Remember, as a girl matures, her body will be changing, so don't forget that the goal with all physical affection is to make her *feel comfortable*—and anything that doesn't meet that goal is, by definition, *inappropriate.*) Holding hands or scratching her back are good starters for the amateur. Spontaneous is good too: Throwing a hug in here and there, without a reason, never seems to be unappreciated at my house. Save the arm punching and choke holds for your boys. Tenderness is what your daughter understands.

Don't let anyone make you feel awkward about being gentle and affectionate with your girls. An affectionate father is a strong father. And strong fathers make confident daughters.

THINK ABOUT IT. . .

- Words may fail, but touch says it all. That's why caring for babies doesn't depend on their vocabulary.

- Some girls are more reluctant to be touched, or more particular about the circumstances; remember to learn the "rules" for each daughter. If your daughter always pulls away from you, or avoids you, you need to change your approach.

TAKING INVENTORY

> Do you touch your daughter in a way that encourages her? Or does she pull back because she's not sure whether she can trust you?

> I had to relearn some things about touching my wife, and that's where I learned the principle of making her comfortable. Growing up, she never could relax around her dad, because his idea of touch was poking, tickling, and then getting mad because his daughters never found it funny.

69. VERBAL AFFECTION IS JUST AS IMPORTANT AS PHYSICAL AFFECTION

Girls love to hear that they're beautiful, talented, smart, funny, helpful, and cool. (You don't have to cover the whole list every time, but make sure to work some variety into your praise. That shows you're paying attention.) We all like to be told good stuff about ourselves, of course. But telling your daughter she's the greatest is only the beginning; *how* you say it also matters.

Tone of voice can either be an artist's brush or monkey droppings. Either way, it's going to leave a mark. If you're aware of this, you will know whether you've left a lasting stroke of beauty on your precious little canvas, or if you are just a poo-flinging primate with a hairy back. I know *content* is important, but that's not the point here. We're talking about affectionate speech, and that means *tone*. So if you are a drill sergeant by nature, given to precise, impersonal discharges of information, or just a sarcastic jerk (my favorite), then you will need to learn to "touch" your daughter gently with your words. In fact, if you don't, you may find that your physical affection is less and less welcomed by her.

Remember the last time you ticked off your wife with a curt response? Did she appreciate being touched after that? Wasn't it chilly enough to frost a beer mug? Well, it's a girl thing, and that's a fact. Your little girl is looking for affirmation from her big strong dad, 24/7. It might seem a tad self-absorbed, but that's the deal. It can be tough not to fling your words like a thoughtless chimp, especially when you're tired. But just keep in mind that, long after the content is forgotten, the tone will be remembered.

A gentle answer turns away wrath,
But a harsh word stirs up anger.
PROVERBS 15:1

Pleasant words are a honeycomb,
Sweet to the soul and healing to the bones.
PROVERBS 16:24

OUR TRANSLATION

> Harsh words get what they deserve. But gentle, pleasant words make everyone feel better; they calm the soul.

THINK ABOUT IT. . .

- Do you allow anyone to speak to your daughter harshly? Of course not! But if you don't hold yourself to that same standard, you're going to be the only name on the butt-kicking list.

- How much of what you think needs to be "fixed" in your daughter really does? And isn't it more important for your daughter to grow than be fixed?

TAKING INVENTORY

> Do you need to apologize for any harsh words from the past week?

> What is the hardest topic for you to talk about without your blood pressure making your tone rise? What your daughter wears? Who she spends time with? Her homework habits? Pay attention to the hot buttons.

70. LAY OUT YOUR RULES FOR DATING LONG BEFORE THE DATING YEARS

You'd better get a head start, my friend. Once the season of young womanhood is upon you, you'll be blown away by the sheer pace of her affections. You need to lay some groundwork so you can say, "Remember what Daddy always said about dating? Not until you're thirty-eight."

Daughters raised in the right environment will always be thinking ahead to dating and marriage, because it's the norm. One of my daughters wanted to play "wedding" at age four, and I was the pretend groom. I'm glad she had such high standards! Girls develop romantic interests so far ahead of boys (thank God) that you can start framing the dating questions almost as soon as you can think of them. Then, when the time comes, you'll have set some expectations in place rather than trying to create them on the fly. This is definitely not a subject on which you want to shoot from the hip.

You and your wife need to be on the same page with this topic more than almost anything else. It is too powerful a force to withstand alone. Any crack in the firewall and your little darling will hit you with everything she's got. And don't worry about being too strict. Better to err on the side of caution than to be too lax—unless you want to deal with a lot of problems. Start communicating a reasonable, but lofty set of expectations as soon as your princess realizes that boys are not just ugly girls. It will make the inevitable more sensible for all involved.

THINK ABOUT IT. . .

 I'm a big believer in clear communication. But it needs to start with your wife. If you aren't together on the topic of dating, it's going to be a bumpy, loud, painful ride. You and your wife should consider your own experiences in dating as the initial guideline. There will be some over-my-dead-body items on each of your lists; the rest is up for negotiation. All this should be done before communicating to your daughter.

TAKING INVENTORY

> What is a nonnegotiable for you when it comes to your daughter's dating? Gang membership? College age or older? Tattooed neck or face? A guy who honks and expects his date to come out to the car?

> What do you think is an appropriate age to begin dating?

> What are your criteria for the guy? Do you have to know him and his family first?

> What are the boundaries on where they're allowed to go, what they're allowed to do, and what time your daughter has to be home?

> Is your daughter allowed to ride in the car with a boy if he's only had his license for a month?

> Is the prom an exception? (Don't be surprised by this one like I was: Some guys will ask a girl to the prom as a first date!)

> CREATURE FROM ANOTHER PLANET <

71. LISTEN TO HER, NO MATTER HOW TIRED YOU ARE, OR HOW TIRED SHE MAKES YOU

Some dads consider it normal, even healthy, if their daughters talk exclusively to their moms, sisters, or other women. Though all those sources are important, you, as her father, are *irreplaceable*. No one can give a girl quite the same sense of importance as her daddy.

But I know how it goes: You come home tired from work with only one thing on your mind—well, three things that dovetail into one: dinner, TV, and quiet. And then your four-year-old daughter wants you to know how she played with her dolls all day by doing a near perfect reenactment. As she peppers you with, "Daddy, look!" and "Daddy, listen!" your brain begins to glaze over.

Not that she isn't the cutest little princess in the world; but at this point in the day, you're not really *in* this world. Just try to remember that her talking to you is the highest compliment she can give. She has been waiting all day to let you know something you missed. How thoughtful! Besides it could be worse. . .teenagers do their talking late at night.

I am usually ready to go to bed by ten. Not that I ever get there that early, but I dream of it. My teenage daughter, on the other hand, is a night owl. Her ideas and hopes spring to life just about the time I peak in my hatred of all forms of energy and sound. She pops in when I am reading or dozing off to announce that she's thinking about becoming a chef, but wonders how she will stay on her diet. . .and what do I know about net carbs and does chocolate really count as a legitimate food group in Switzerland?

Daughters are sensitive about how they're received. Your reluctance to listen to *whatever* she has to say, *whenever* it comes up, could develop into a reluctance on her part to talk to you the next time—and that time might be the time when she asks about a guy's inappropriate behavior, or her best friend trying to get her to try "recreational" drugs. As dads, we can't afford to miss the big and serious questions because we didn't build up the habit of listening to the little quirky ones.

A WORD FROM THE WORD

This you know, my beloved brethren. But everyone must be quick to hear, slow to speak and slow to anger.
JAMES 1:19

OUR TRANSLATION

> You can add to the list "slow to show irritability because you'd rather be doing something else."

THINK ABOUT IT. . .

- Listening is a God-like trait. The more we practice it ourselves, the more we show the Father to our family, especially to our kids.

- The act of listening is an act of love—one that will endure in the years to come.

- The younger a girl is, the less she's able to recognize "extenuating circumstances" and let you off the hook because you've had a hard day. She will interpret that as "he doesn't want to listen."

72. CELEBRATE HER FIRST PERIOD WITH DIGNITY

OK, wow. Thankfully, somebody warned me about this one. Here is perhaps the most befuddling thing a dad can face. Your little girl, your princess, your scooterbug, is about to cross a major threshold into womanhood. She will quickly and suddenly become someone new—and occasionally moody and scary. But that's just the female species for you. Her mom, sister, or close female friend may have already begun to prepare her for this awesome blessing from God. But who's preparing Dad? It's a big day for you too!

So here it is.

First, you will need to be on alert, maybe for an entire year. There is such a wide range of ages when girls get their period that you will just need to be patient. Also, you will need an informant: probably your wife, but it could be a sister or even a teacher. Most likely, they will know first and will need to let you know ASAP when things change.

I was at work when my wife called to let me know about our first daughter. On the way home, I stopped at the store and bought a half-dozen white roses for her, one red rose for my wife, and flowers for my daughter's best friend, who was there, and my younger daughter. When I walked in the door and saw that my daughter had been crying, I just handed her the roses and hugged her. All I could squeak out was, "I'm so proud of you."

I distributed the other flowers with more hugs and no speeches or comments. We went on with our normal routine, except surrounded by flowers! It was an affirmation from her daddy that becoming a woman was a good thing, and not a hurdle for her or for our relationship.

If you worry that your informant might not get to you in time, I strongly suggest that you buy a special gift in advance and keep it hidden for that moment—but probably not flowers, because they will die. Don't try to "celebrate" by going out to do something, because the very nature of the event will not lend itself to that. Just be aware of the dignity and meaning of the experience for your daughter and you will make it a holy thing for her forever.

BONUS THOUGHT

How menstruation was discussed or addressed, if at all, when you were growing up will likely be your own basis for acknowledging it in your daughter's life. My own household was dead silent about it. We men did not want to know or understand it. That made it even more imperative that I not pass on my inherent awkwardness to my girls. I didn't want to communicate some kind of shame attached to her God-given femininity. That is something we dads cannot afford to do.

TAKING INVENTORY

> What ages are your daughters?

> Are you and your wife on the same page about this issue, and is she willing to help you with an appropriate response?

> Has your daughter already had her first period and you missed the opportunity? (You can still recover by treating her with dignity when the next event comes. But instead of a landmark event, make it a quiet, but special thing, something considerate and thoughtful.)

> Have you spent some time considering how you will prepare for this rite of passage in your daughter's life?

73. COMPLIMENT HER IN FRONT OF OTHERS

There's nothing we all love more than a real compliment—except maybe money (or that could just be me). Yep, apart from an unexpected cash windfall, I'd rather get a pat on the back more than just about anything. The affirmation goes straight to the heart. The only thing that makes it better is doing it in front of other people.

Your daughter will eat this up while pretending to be mortified. She'll tell you, "Stop!" and, "Dad, you're embarrassing me." But deep down you'll be building her heart up and letting her know where she ranks with you. Just be natural and don't overdo it, or she may think you're about to ask to borrow some money.

If one member suffers, all the members suffer with it;
if one member is honored, all the members rejoice with it.

1 Corinthians 12:26

OUR TRANSLATION

> All the other "members" can't rejoice with the one unless they know about it. That's why publicly praising and complimenting is important.

THINK ABOUT IT. . .

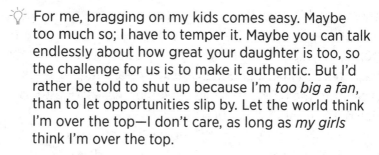 For me, bragging on my kids comes easy. Maybe too much so; I have to temper it. Maybe you can talk endlessly about how great your daughter is too, so the challenge for us is to make it authentic. But I'd rather be told to shut up because I'm *too big a fan*, than to let opportunities slip by. Let the world think I'm over the top—I don't care, as long as *my girls* think I'm over the top.

7 4 . LISTEN TO HER MUSIC IN THE CAR

I know what a sacrifice this can be. I have suffered now for years unwillingly learning the lyrics to songs that are almost as inane as some of the ones I grew up with. (If you can sing along to Rupert Holmes's "Piña Colada," you have no room to criticize the lyrics of your daughter's favorite songs. . .*ever*.)

The goal is to make your time together fun and enjoyable—at least for her; you will suffer. It also makes you seem cooler than you really are. Harmonizing with Bad Company or demonstrating impeccable timing to "Bicycle Race" may have done it in our day, but this is the new millennium. If you don't at least know who Taylor Swift and Bruno Mars are, you're going to be a square forever. Being at least a little bit in touch with your daughter's culture via music makes you more accessible later when you will be dealing with bigger issues.

It also means you can point to real-world examples of what *not* to do. Sadly, my girls and I have tracked more than one young singer as she morphs from adorable child star to cheap *pop-tart*. Watching someone else's little princess self-destruct during her teen years is not entertainment, though you couldn't tell from the ruthless tabloid coverage. But it can be useful as a warning to your own daughters.

Maybe it will cause you to grind your teeth at night, but the next time you get in the car to take your daughter somewhere, ask her what station she wants to listen to. She will appreciate it, and you won't have to argue the point that *the '80s are* not the oldies!

THINK ABOUT IT. . .

- Music has become such a dominant cultural force that to be ignorant of it is to mistake its power in crafting the world our children are growing up in. Better to have some idea of what choices there are out there and direct your girl's interests where possible.

TAKING INVENTORY

> Is there a musical genre you can both agree on? (In our house, country music is the closest to common ground.)

> Have you ever tried to find an artist you both like and take your daughter to a concert?

> Do you "force" your daughter (and the rest of the family) to listen to the news or sports on long trips?

> Have you and your daughter ever tried exploring new music on independent music sites, or streaming music sources like Pandora or Spotify?

75. EAT ANYTHING SHE COOKS FOR YOU WITHOUT COMPLAINT

Despite trends to the contrary, most cooking is still done by the women in the family. Even women with careers outside the home still have more than half the responsibility for preparing meals. And if your wife stays at home, it's more like 99 percent, unless you have a coupon for KFC in your pocket, or, like me, enjoy trying out what you've watched on the Food Channel.

Fortunately, most women take pride in their skills in the kitchen. This is one of the first areas of accomplishment your daughter is going to learn that will directly affect others. Sure, she takes pride in her crayon drawings and dance recitals, but cooking is her big chance to contribute to the family and gain some self-esteem. So chew and smile, no matter how much it tastes like Play-Doh, no matter the lingering burnt aroma, no matter the glue-like texture. She's achieving and learning to serve—a nice combination to learn early in life.

THINK ABOUT IT. . .

 Anything you want your little girl to embrace should be celebrated. During her lifetime, she will do a lot of cooking, for herself and probably for a family one day. Never complain or belittle her first efforts at home. Don't be anything less than enthusiastic. You can tweak her recipes and cooking times later, discreetly. My girls always liked to be my sous chefs when I tried my hand at a gourmet meal. Even if their efforts were less than Iron Chef quality, the experience was fun and bonded us together. Later on, they began to take the lead, and there were some spicy dinners I had to endure while they honed their skills. Keep a bottle of Tums handy and keep on smiling.

76. HANDLE BOY-CRAZINESS WITH CAUTION

Boy-craziness. It's natural. It's inevitable. It's coming to a daughter near you.

Boys are bad news to any dad who once was one. They are going to go through what you and I did—a kind of werewolf movie in slow motion call *adolescence*. And our daughters will be slightly ahead of them. If you have a son, he will be the only boy you can be sure your daughters will hate. The rest are the enemy.

Of course I exaggerate, a little. It's just that the transition for us dads from having little tiny princesses who think boys are yucky (which they are) to having young ladies primping and preparing in front of the mirror for the sake of all those clueless teenage slobs is really tough. It's been much harder for me to see my girls as young women than for them to see it. I'm smack in the middle of the boys-boys-boys phase, and I'm telling you it is fraught with landmines I never imagined. Crushes, infatuations, hurt feelings, insecurities, competition—and, above all, *drama*! This is territory that requires us dads to do several things that don't come naturally, like listening without comment and taking everything seriously—even when it's silly. We can't tease, roll our eyes, or ignore hurts; and, above all, we can't get angry. You will be tempted to straighten out every issue the old-fashioned way, but I encourage you to refrain.

This is a time of discovery for a girl, as her brain and body are being rewired. Your daughter will want your input, but usually not unsolicited. She will come to you if she feels safe. Be involved, but tender. If we dads handle this rite of passage with patience, gentleness, and great caution, our girls will grow in confidence, and develop a healthy view of the opposite sex—of which we are supposed to be the primary model.

I think I need an aspirin.

TAKING INVENTORY

> Does your daughter communicate her feelings about boys to you or your wife?

> Are you and your wife on the same page about how and where your daughter is allowed to interact with boys? For many of us, outside of school, church youth groups were the first arena to get to know the opposite sex. If that's the case, you will have to discuss things like church lock-ins and retreats, and when you think she is ready to attend those.

> The more "generic" her interest, the easier it is to handle it. Boys on TV, boys at the mall, boys at school are less of a concern than that one boy in her English class, the boy down the street, or the brother of her best friend. Does your daughter have her heart set on one boy in particular? Most likely it will be a passing fancy, but don't try to explain that to her—she doesn't have the big picture yet. Be patient. Also be diligent.

77. REMEMBER SPECIAL DAYS BESIDES BIRTHDAYS AND HOLIDAYS

Although men are often accused of being the ones who forget important dates, such as birthdays and anniversaries, women are equally guilty. My wife regularly forgets the first day of football season and the World Championship Punkin Chunkin (as seen on Science Channel), despite the fact that they happen *every* year. So, guys, it's not just us.

But since we are more forgiving, as long as we can find the remote, we men will always be at a disadvantage here. Such is the life of a dad. Better to go ahead and take out your calendar at the beginning of the year and mark down anything your daughter will be targeting. The obvious one beyond her birthday is of course Valentine's Day. That's a no-brainer. Try to think about what she thinks is important. It could be something serious like Veteran's Day, because you or her mom serves in the military; or the anniversary of a grandparent's passing remembered with a trip to place flowers on the grave. It could be a much lighter occasion, such as her sixth grade graduation or high school prom.

But girls also have some unusual ideas about special days to celebrate, and these you will have to figure out on a per-daughter basis. Some girls think spring has a starting day to be celebrated by shopping. Some celebrate "monthiversaries" when they start dating. Some think their best friend's special days will flow onto your family's calendar. It's totally subjective, but nonetheless important to your daughter. Just don't forget the ones you know are coming, and keep a stash of iTunes and Starbucks gift cards for the ones that hit you when you thought you were safe.

THINK ABOUT IT...

 It's easier as a team to identify these kinds of "other" special days. Ask your wife to help you keep up. Also, older daughters are a wealth of information on their younger sisters. Maybe casually bring up special days for the upcoming month over dinner, then quietly put them into your calendar. Imagine your daughter's delight when you show up with flowers the day she gets her license, or with a box of chocolates for her to share with her best friend who just got accepted to college. It tells her you understand and value the way she sees the world.

78. WATCH HER WARDROBE CLOSELY

Unfortunately, as your daughter grows up, her wardrobe will get tighter in the most worrisome places. You don't want her to go from sweetheart to sweet tart, so it's better to start establishing the definition of *modest* when she doesn't care about labels or style, only that it's bright pink and lime green. Moms are good communicators of standards, of course, but don't underestimate your role as an opinion giver. In fact, if you follow our earlier advice and take your daughter shopping every once in a while, you'll have earned some cred so that your comments won't seem out of place. Let me rephrase that: Your comments won't seem *as* out of place.

The heads-up here is that the world around us is fighting to sexualize our little girls *years* before they're ready. Your involvement with her on that topic may be limited until the issue of modesty comes up at the mall. Be gentle—I urge you from my own mistakes! But be prepared. Your daughter wants to feel *feminine*, not necessarily sexy. That's a good thing, and can be encouraged with a little patience and some education on women's styles. Identify stores that offer things more along the lines you find acceptable, and buy your daughter a gift card to those stores. It will help *stir* her rather than *drag* her to better choices. Clearly communicate any absolutes about whatever you (and your wife) will not accept. Listen to the adult women in your life, too, so that your fashion opinions don't get stuck in past decades. In short, be involved. Your guidance matters.

I want women to adorn themselves with proper clothing, modestly and discreetly, not with braided hair and gold or pearls or costly garments, but rather by means of good works, as is proper for women making a claim to godliness.

1 Timothy 2:9–10

OUR TRANSLATION

> Note: This verse is dangerous. First, it's directed toward grown women; second, it's in the context of the first-century Roman world. But the point is still valid: *modesty* and *discretion* are important. What that looks like from culture to culture, and from generation to generation will vary widely.

THINK ABOUT IT. . .

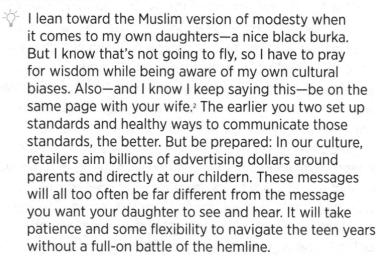

I lean toward the Muslim version of modesty when it comes to my own daughters—a nice black burka. But I know that's not going to fly, so I have to pray for wisdom while being aware of my own cultural biases. Also—and I know I keep saying this—be on the same page with your wife.[2] The earlier you two set up standards and healthy ways to communicate those standards, the better. But be prepared: In our culture, retailers aim billions of advertising dollars around parents and directly at our childern. These messages will all too often be far different from the message you want your daughter to see and hear. It will take patience and some flexibility to navigate the teen years without a full-on battle of the hemline.

---

2. I am keenly aware that some dads are divorced or otherwise single. I know you face greater hurdles when it comes to being on the same page with your daughter's mom (provided she's in the picture). But if you can partner with a significant female voice in your daughter's life—an aunt, grandmother, teacher—you will fare better than being alone on this one. After all, what does a *dad* know about women's fashion?

79. WATCH OUT FOR HER FIRST BROKEN HEART

It's coming, and there's no way to stop it. No matter how scary and threatening you are, some guy is going to catch your daughter's attention, and because of simple immaturity he's going to crush her romantic expectations. This kid is probably not even going to know he did it. That makes it really hard to justify beating him into unconsciousness. That, and the probability that he will be under fourteen, and no smarter about girls than you were at that age. In the big picture, his painful departure from your daughter's life is actually a blessing, because you don't want her getting serious at this age anyway. The tough part for you as a dad will be that conflicted feeling of tearing his face off and thanking him for getting out of her life.

The tough part for her will be the sense of rejection. Call it puppy love if you want to, but the first time she has her heart broken, she'll feel like a Rottweiler bit into it. With some perspective, it may become a melodramatic comedy later for both of you. But that's *later*.

When it happens, remember above all else not to treat her dented romantic feelings lightly! Girls hurt at that age in direct proportion to their innocence. And don't forget that these experiences are building steam for later. Each one hits a little harder and hurts a little more. You need to be someone she runs to for consolation in romance, since you are the only man she can truly trust.

BONUS THOUGHT

Recently, a guy I work with asked me about how to handle some breakup fallout with his twelve-year-old daughter. He admitted he thought the whole thing was silly, but wondered what I thought. Coincidentally, his daughter had also recently suffered a broken ankle. I asked him if he was impatient with her while she wore her cast, and if he thought it was silly to limp from the pain as she recovered. Of course he said *no*. I asked him why he would treat a broken heart any differently than a broken ankle. Neither were her fault and both hurt terribly. So why would they not both take time to heal? He pretty much thought I was awesome after that.

80. BRAG ABOUT HER WHEN SHE THINKS YOU DON'T KNOW SHE'S LISTENING

When you live with people, you overhear stuff, whether you like it or not. Lives overlap like dirty laundry on a teenager's floor. That means you are going to be apologizing or explaining—*often*. Or you may suffer the consequences of some dumb remark and never, ever know that was the cause. I say, *why not make some positive use of this otherwise negative force?* I know it sounds a little calculated, but I *try* to be overheard when it's something I want my daughters to know I really believe. For some reason, saying it to them directly is considered suspect. I'm just being their dad. But let them think they've overheard something that wasn't meant for their ears and it instantly becomes reality.

That's why I like to brag about my girls when they think I don't know they're within earshot. When friends or family come over, I might talk a little louder about how talented my girls are, so they can hear it from upstairs. I might mention how well they are doing in school while I'm on the phone outside their door. Almost any time they are around the corner or down the hall, I'll use my "outdoor voice" to tell my wife how beautiful my daughters are.

Bragging is a compliment to your girls, at any age. After all, it would be selfish of me not to let the world in on such a good thing. And it can't hurt my girls to eavesdrop on a man who is unapologetically their biggest fan.

BONUS THOUGHT

Don't confuse healthy bragging with flattery. What I'm suggesting is letting your daughter know your honest feelings in a way that doesn't bring her guard up. Self-consciousness is about as common a female trait as there is, so letting her hear you brag at a safe distance gives her some cover. Don't lay it on thick—just be honest, and loud.

81. DON'T OVERREACT TO MELTDOWNS

Girls. What is going on inside those seemingly sweet little heads? Not much a man would ever understand from his own upbringing. (It's hard enough to even remember my own upbringing.) But daughters are truly from another planet when it comes to emotional overload.

Starting from the earliest stages, men learn to deal with emotions through a mechanism known as *inappropriate behavior*. It's oh so convenient, because it can be practiced anywhere under any circumstances, from weddings to the workplace. Tantrums, foul language, aggressive posturing—all these outlets allow men to vent their emotions without actually feeling them. Life is good.

But girls are not so conveniently wired. They actually work through their feelings or burst into tears or have "episodes." Sometimes all at once. They find this meltdown cathartic and healthy, while you and I, as dads, find it confusing and annoying. There's no handle to grab, no nail to drive, no parts to glue. We'll be frustrated and on edge because the desire to *fix* what's wrong will be pouring over us while they're simply using us as a captive audience for the drama of their unraveling lives.

My only encouragement here is to *wait*, and don't overreact. Wait it out like a thunderstorm on the interstate. Keep your hands on the wheel and stare straight ahead. Be patient; any sudden reaction could spell disaster. Girls need for us to give them a stage to work out the overload—and, only if invited, offer advice or step in.

OUR TRANSLATION

> The apostle Paul had no problem using a feminine metaphor to describe himself and how his team approached their work. As driven as he was to see change, he took the time it required to make sure he didn't break anything on the way to fixing it.

THINK ABOUT IT...

Girls take time. Period. And they frequently process their thoughts verbally, soaked with emotion. They don't see it that way, of course, but then they don't see much of anything the way we dads do. They need a patient listener. But here's the really good news for dad: If you keep your mouth shut long enough for your daughter to work things out, you'll come out looking like Father of the Year. So shut up, and be successful.

82. HELP HER RECOGNIZE "FEMININE COMPETITION"

This, I readily admit, was something my wife had to educate me about. It started years ago when she opened my eyes to the fact that women dress to impress other women. Of course I thought I'd heard her wrong, but she was patient with me. Apparently, the opinions of *other women* are more important than the opinions of men. It took me a while, but after considering the quality of my comments on all things female, I conceded her point. But she wasn't done with me so easily.

Thus began my reeducation on the world my daughters were born into: the world where feminine competition makes ESPN look like a knitting festival. I'm not referring to healthy competition, either. Girls can and should play sports with all the same gusto that boys do, and learn to win or lose appropriately. No, the kind of competition my wife clued me in on is the kind that makes for unnecessary drama, poor character, and broken relationships. It can even be considered a spiritual shortcoming as a girl gets older. It's the kind of competition that has undue influence on her self-worth—and shaping self-worth is part of *our* job as dads.

As a dad, if you are aware of this kind of competition when it pops up, you can gently guide your daughter away from the whole mess and into areas of real substance. The key is recognizing those moments when you see your daughter gauging her self-worth against the other girls around her. It's simple in concept, but subtle in most instances. Watch for behavioral changes around other girls, such as withdrawing or becoming more assertive than normal. Both often indicate that there is a battle in her mind about how she compares to others, whether good or bad. She will likely not be able to articulate it, so be cautious about asking deep questions too quickly. I like to try to balance those competitive moments by giving good old-fashioned fatherly attention. Timing is everything, and injecting a little *genuine* self-esteem into the emotions she's feeling can often calm the storm inside. Guiding her to take a more spiritual interest in her "competitors" can also make your girl aware that comparing herself to them is a waste of time.

Don't worry that you can't fix every instance. Comparing her looks, her body type, and her clothing style come all too naturally—so be patient. (Seems like *patience* is a word that keeps popping up in this book!) Helping your little darling to build others up rather than comparing and competing with them will save her a world of insecurity and drama later. She'll become the girl that other girls feel safe around.

Start with the truth that God made her special, and you as her dad are here to make sure she never forgets it—no matter what her hair looks like. And, by the way, to prove it to her, she just might need another hairbrush.

THINK ABOUT IT. . .

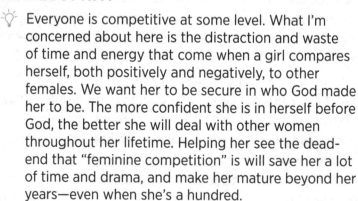

Everyone is competitive at some level. What I'm concerned about here is the distraction and waste of time and energy that come when a girl compares herself, both positively and negatively, to other females. We want her to be secure in who God made her to be. The more confident she is in herself before God, the better she will deal with other women throughout her lifetime. Helping her see the dead-end that "feminine competition" is will save her a lot of time and drama, and make her mature beyond her years—even when she's a hundred.

83. LET HER PICK OUT YOUR COLOGNE

Your daughter's opinion ought to matter to you. She certainly thinks it should. Training her to make good decisions before the big issues come up is important. Trusting her to make decisions that affect you personally can be powerful...and sometimes powerful smelling.

Take your daughter to the fragrance counter at the mall, but instead of telling her what perfume you like for her, switch things around: Let her pick out a cologne for you. Women have better olfactory senses than men anyway, and assuming you're not wearing cologne for the guys at your office or at the gym, your daughter may very well pick one that the women around you will notice. (Not many of us married men would admit that we care what "other" women think.) In any case, letting her choose something for you tells her that her opinion matters. In fact, it matters so much that you're willing to wear it in public.

84. IF SHE WON'T SHARE THE INNER THINGS, BE THERE FOR THE OUTER THINGS

Many girls, especially as they enter puberty, feel much more comfortable talking to Mom, a sister, or an aunt, than to Dad. Basically anything in a skirt has more credibility than a man. It's because they're turning into women, for better or worse.

Some dads feel left out during this time, and some are glad to be left out. Some are frustrated they aren't included, and some are happily absent. But in most cases, it's not really up to you or me. And that's okay. Let your daughter's need for girl talk find its own level of comfort. If she includes you in this amazing and frightening process, be sensitive and mostly quiet.

If, however, your daughter puts a "No Boys Allowed" sign on her heart—like my girls did—don't let that stop you. If you are *left out* of the inner things, make sure to be *in* on the outer things. There's plenty of stuff you can be involved in without intruding where she's not inviting you. Talk about her day, the last song she bought, what she thinks she'd like for her first car. Talk about the flippin' weather if you have to, but don't play the strong silent role in everything. As she grows through this time of life, you can probe her comfort level about sharing deeper things by asking soft questions. Just be prepared to be told to "butt out," and don't get your fragile little feelings hurt.

A WORD FROM THE WORD

A plan in the heart of a man is like deep water,
But a man of understanding draws it out.
PROVERBS 20:5

OUR TRANSLATION

> Being a man of understanding often feels like powerlessness at first. But a man of understanding isn't one who dives in to fix things, or to make his point. He takes the time necessary to draw things out of others. And when it comes to his own daughter, he really takes his time with the "deep water" so he doesn't get in over his head.

85. LET HER TEACH YOU SOMETHING

As your little princess matures, be prepared for what inevitably comes next: She will actually know more than you do about some topics. When that happens, how will you deal with it? Your daughter will be watching for your reaction—and your wife will be enjoying every last minute of it.

Recently, my eldest daughter moved home after graduating from college. We both work, watch TV at night, eat on a regular basis, and need to exercise. Since my orthopedist had cautioned that my basketball days are over, I jumped at the chance to play in a coed volleyball league at a coworker's church. (Granted, I don't jump as high as I used to.) My daughter and two high school girls are also on our team, playing alongside their dads—three old guys who "carry," misdirect, and generally flub the ball way too often. (Had I listened to my daughters' coaching about my incorrect hits when we'd occasionally play throughout the years, I wouldn't just now be learning how to hit the ball correctly. But, alas, I didn't listen. I made excuses, and now I'm constantly waiting for the ref to blow the whistle and point at me for the whole gym to see. My self-image takes a beating every week.)

What can you learn from your daughter? For starters, here are some things she might be able to teach you:

> The lingo in all the Harry Potter books

> What is happening in the movie that you don't understand because you didn't read the book

> How to Tweet or Instagram

> What's wrong with your wireless router

> Who might win the Academy Awards this year—and who probably should win

> What your wife is really thinking

Your daughter has much to teach you. Are you listening?

TAKING INVENTORY

> On a scale of one to ten, how are you doing as a listener?

> What can you do to sharpen your listening skills?

> Make a list of ten things your daughter can teach you right now. Then set up an appointment with her and tell her she is the teacher and you're the eager student.

86. KEEP DATING HER IN HIGH SCHOOL AND BEYOND

Earlier, we talked about the need to date your daughter. Here's the really cool thing about doing that when she's young. She may still want to hang out with you when she gets older. That is something you should definitely not take for granted. Some of my proudest moments as a dad were in my daughters' high school years. A time or two when they were asked to go somewhere with a friend, their response was, "I can't. I've already promised to go with my dad to a movie." They might have been on the phone in their bedroom and I overheard the conversation from another room—but I beamed with great delight each time. Could it be they had no money to go out with friends and they knew I was buying? Sure, but that's beside the point. For just a few moments in those high school years, my time with them was the most important thing on their agenda. Wow. That's huge!

When Disney released *The Princess and the Frog* in theaters, my twenty-something daughter and I went on a date. We did what we always do. We bought our Milk Duds and Mike and Ike's ahead of time, and she snuck them into the theater in her purse. Then we bought the large popcorn combo (the one that costs more than the tickets, but it includes refillable drinks and a refillable tub). As we took our seats in the front, where we could put our feet on the railing, she leaned over and whispered to me, "Daddy, this is just like the very first movie you ever took me to—*The Little Mermaid*." As I silenced my cell phone and prepared for the previews, I turned my head away from her and choked back the tears— just like I did at her very first movie.

If you open the door for her when she gets in the car and when you walk into the theater to purchase your tickets, she'll know what she should expect when other guys (who aren't good enough for her) take her out on dates. Moral of the story: date her early, date her often.

TAKING INVENTORY

> What are some of the best dates you've ever had with your daughter? What made them so good?

> What kinds of things would she like to do on a date with you now? Plan one or two dates very soon.

> What kinds of things do you need to model for your daughter on a date?

87. TEACH HER HOW TO DRIVE

You need to teach your daughter how to drive two kinds of things: a golf ball from a tee box, and a car. We'll talk about golf later. Yes, you should probably send her to an accredited driving school, and your wife may have a better driving record than you do, but there's something about a dad teaching his daughter what it feels like to get behind the wheel. This may have started long ago when a caveman first discovered the wheel and his teenage daughter quickly figured out that she also needed to learn how to roll it correctly—something she might be able to do to impress Og and his friends at the mall. And so the tradition continues today.

I recommend starting her off in a big empty parking lot. For both of my daughters, I began at our church's lot on a night when very few people were there. We only needed to avoid curbs, light poles, and the church building itself, and there was ample room for big, sweeping turns to be made. On both occasions, I was prepared for the natural tendency of teenage girls to slam on the brakes and propel their dad through the windshield. In contrast to most teenage guys, girls are more prone to be afraid to press the gas pedal too hard, so we needed to work on getting the right feel for the pedal and what speed she'd need to maintain in order not to get pulled over by a cop or passed by a grandma. We also worked on parking between the lines—something they were very interested in learning, as it is a necessity for going shopping!

After my daughters mastered the church parking lot, it was time to head out for a test run on a road where they would encounter other drivers. . .a defining moment for both them and me. I still remember the initial looks of sheer horror on their faces—thankfully, we got through it. We graduated to a highway, where we could increase our speed, and I chose to take them during a time that provided the fewest obstacles (also known as other motorists). By the time they both began their driving school training, they felt much more confident about the task at hand, which is the ultimate goal for what can be a bone-chilling, finger-biting experience for everyone.

Additionally, whether she wants to or not, a girl needs to be familiar with why you should change the oil in a car every so often, where the spare tire and jack are located, what the "service engine soon" light means, how to put air in the tires, why she shouldn't talk on her cell phone or text while she drives, and why the car should be washed with some frequency. Most of these things will not be passed on to her by her mother, which is another reason why you must be the one to teach her all about driving. . .and all the responsibilities that accompany that privilege. Perhaps the biggest warning I should pass along is this: After she becomes an expert at this thing you've been doing for years, she'll be quick to point out what a bad driver you actually are. Good luck with *that*.

A WORD FROM THE WORD

Give me understanding and I will obey your instructions;
I will put them into practice with all my heart.
PSALM 119:34 NLT

TAKING INVENTORY

> In the past, how has the interchange gone between you as the instructor and your daughter as the learner? What has gone well? What needs improvement?

> What practical tips do you need to pass on to your girl in regard to proper car maintenance?

> Do you need to ask God for patience before embarking on this job? Any other requests you need to ask of him?

88. TRY NOT TO EMBARRASS HER

More than once, upon hearing of something stupid a friend of mine has done in front of his daughter, I have been heard to say, "Hey, we've earned the right to embarrass ourselves in front of our kids. It's what dads do." There are various levels of embarrassment, however, and I propose that we at least give it a shot to avoid the worst-case scenarios.

I still remember how one of my nieces would warn her sister when she and her dad were coming to pick her up from a party. "Come out of the house quickly, before Dad gets out of the car. He's wearing *those* sweatpants and his house slippers." You didn't need to tell her sister twice. Perhaps that's exactly *why* he wore those clothes when he picked her up! Not a bad idea, unless you wind up in an accident on the way home. . .and then I hope he had on clean underwear!

One of our youngest daughter's best friends is Jewish. She hopes to become a rabbi someday. Her family invited my daughter and me to their house to observe Passover a few years ago, and I accepted with great anticipation. We had celebrated "a Christian Passover" with a few small groups from church in times past, and I was anxious to see how our observances compared with the real deal. Plus, having studied Hebrew for a whole semester in Bible college back in the day, I was hoping to see how my pronunciation fared among a Jewish family who spoke the language at Shabbat services each week.

Meanwhile, my daughter had other thoughts that she had expressed to me. She hoped I wouldn't "embarrass myself" by having too much of the Manischewitz wine, asking inappropriate questions about religion, talking with my mouth full, or generally getting into people's space. Real concerns, all. By the grace of God, I managed to pass the test.

We dads *will* embarrass ourselves in front of our daughters from time to time. Especially during their teenage years. It's somehow in our DNA. But the best we can hope for is to minimize the embarrassment in front of her friends. She may at least give you some credit if she knows you are sincerely trying.

A WORD FROM THE WORD

Out of respect for Christ,
be courteously reverent to one another.
EPHESIANS 5:21 MSG

TAKING INVENTORY

> Can you think of a time when you embarrassed your daughter by something you did or said? What could you have done differently in that situation?

> How can you show respect to your daughter when you are around her friends?

> If she gives you permission to embarrass yourself in a particular situation, go for it with all your might!

89. SCRAPBOOK WITH HER

When my daughters graduated from high school, they got a lot of nice gifts from friends and family. Their favorites? Money, of course! But the gift their friends probably enjoyed the most was one that I gave to each of them. A sixty-two-page (12" x 12") scrapbook that chronicled their lives up to that point. And their friends were heard to question at each of their graduation parties, "Your *dad* made this?" I'm secure in my masculinity. Absolutely!

Contrary to popular belief, scrapbooking is not just for women. It is, in fact, a hobby that some men enjoy. Anyone who is creative and enjoys using the right side of his brain has the potential to be a scrapper. I give all the credit to my wife for getting me started. She knew I liked design, and enjoyed watching a good book come together. So, the winter before our eldest daughter graduated, my wife organized the photos from our daughter's birth, through elementary and junior high, into high school. Pictures of her trips to Mamaw and Papaw's, the zoo, dance recitals, softball games, school plays, her baptism, achievements and awards, and pictures of Christmases—lots of Christmases.

I became a frequent shopper at places like Michael's, Hobby Lobby, and Archiver's; and I discovered lots of cool and colorful paper, embellishments, 3-D stickers, chipboard letters, and more. I took notes from a scrapbook mentor of mine, and have even joined in a few all-female scrap-a-thons. (Did you know they *eat* at those things?) Ultimately, though, I forged my own style.

For the next three months, I spent many late nights working on the scrapbook that our daughter would get when she graduated. Then I did it all over again two years later for our younger daughter. I knew it had become an obsession when I promised another guy at work I would buy his lunch if he would use a coupon from the newspaper to get me 40 percent off one big item, while I used my own coupon at the same store.

And now scrapbooking is a family affair. My wife and I fight with our daughters for square footage on the kitchen table. One of the bookcases in my office at home has even been converted into Scrapbook Central. I know a few other guys (okay, one) who have discovered how much fun—and expensive—this hobby can be. If you choose to follow my lead and go for it in this uncharted territory for manly men, here are some benefits you will reap:

> As you look through photos and recall some great memories with your daughter, you will experience them all over again—as many times as you like.

> Your daughter will discover that you are not too cool to break out of the mold and do something creative and artsy.

> Her friends will see how much you care about your daughter.

> You may even discover a hobby you can do with your wife after your days on the baseball diamond are over.

> You may get some really cool tools as Christmas presents. (My mother-in-law buys the best ones!)

> When you've had a really bad week at work, you might discover how therapeutic this hobby can be.

So, go ahead and scrapbook with her. I dare you.

TAKING INVENTORY

> Can you think of other examples in the Bible where God used the artistry and craftmanship of men to accomplish his purposes?

> If you're not ready to take the leap into scrapbooking, what is some other kind of crafty activity you could participate in with your daughter?

> Are there other things that might be more therapeutic for you? What are they, and how can you participate in them with your daughter?

90. TAKE HER TO A MAJOR SPORTING EVENT

Some guys have it easy. . .their girls just automatically love sports. But even if you're not one of those guys, there is still hope!

If you've done your job early in your daughter's life, by attending Girl Scout dances and sitting through piano and dance recitals, then you may have a shot at getting your daughter to enjoy watching sporting events with you. At the very least, maybe you can convince the female population in your house to take you to a professional baseball game on Father's Day. Every girl needs to learn how to keep score at a ball game—and besides, it's one of the best ways to keep your little girl occupied between the first inning hot dog, third inning trip to the bathroom, fifth inning soft pretzel, seventh inning bathroom trip, and eighth inning ice cream sundae in a baseball helmet. (If it goes into extra innings, it will take bribery on your part to get her to stay!) Coaches will be impressed years later when they are in need of an official scorekeeper, and your daughter (now a mom with her own daughter) is the one who steps up to keep the book.

If you're really lucky, like I was, you might even be able to take your girl to some college hockey games, a pro football game, or the NCAA Final Four. *Think I'm just dreaming?* Not so. A few years ago, I picked up my daughter after work on a Monday and we drove the four-and-a-half hours to Ford Field in Detroit to see the North Carolina basketball team annihilate Michigan State before a record crowd of 72,922. We've watched a lot of college basketball in our house, and for whatever reason (perhaps the light blue color of UNC's uniforms) my daughter has always been a huge fan of the Tar Heels. She felt that Tyler Hansbrough was her "soul mate." So when a friend called on Sunday and told me he had two tickets for the championship game the next night that I could purchase at face value, my wife immediately responded, "You have to figure out how to get there. Your daughter is a huge Tar Heel fan." (Props to my wife for the nudge!)

I called my daughter later that afternoon and mentioned the possibility to her. In response, I heard nothing but silence—as in *shock*—followed by this: "Daddy, if you take me, I'll love you forever!" To which I responded, "I thought you already loved me forever!" The road trip simply sealed the deal.

We listened to "One Shining Moment" and other songs she had downloaded on our road mix for the way up I-75. And as we sat there, she in her Carolina blue T-shirt surrounded by a sea of Michigan State green, whispering to me that we might not want to cheer loud, I responded, "We paid good money for these tickets. . .trust me, we will cheer!" It is a memory we will never forget. North Carolina 89, Michigan State 72. How do I know the score? We scrapbooked it!

A WORD FROM THE WORD

You've all been to the stadium and seen the athletes race.
Everyone runs; one wins. Run to win. All good athletes train hard.
They do it for a gold medal that tarnishes and fades.
You're after one that's gold eternally.
1 CORINTHIANS 9:24–25 MSG

TAKING INVENTORY

> What are some of your best road-trip memories with your daughter?

> What is an event about which your daughter might say to you, "Daddy, if you take me, I'll love you forever!"? Can you get tickets?

> By taking your daughter to a sporting event with you, what kinds of things are you saying to her?

91. TAKE HER FOR LONG WALKS ON THE BEACH

If you take your family on vacation every summer, chances are you'll end up on the beach in South Carolina, Georgia, or Florida a time or two. Perhaps the Gulf Coast or southern California. There is no better place for taking a good, long walk with your daughter than on the beach.

As our girls were growing up, I made this a practice every year that we were anywhere near sand. Sometimes we walked down the beach to play volleyball together. At times, we headed down the coast to catch a concert or a sandcastle-building contest, or to jump in the pool at a really cool resort or buy slushes from a vendor on the beach. On days when we were really lucky, we watched as several dolphins jumped and frolicked not far from the beach. All the while, we talked about life. . .in elementary school. . .in junior high. . .in high school.

A funny thing happened as my girls grew older. I noticed more and more guys starting to check them out. As I glared at the oglers, my daughters and I continued to talk. Then, during their teenage years, when we talked about purity (how they should dress and what guys are thinking) I could refer back to those moments. I vividly remember the day when my younger daughter quoted our youth pastor's wife concerning the plight of guys' visual obsession: "I don't know whether to be disgusted with you guys or feel sympathy for you!" That's a discussion for another day.

A WORD FROM THE WORD

Be very sure now, you who have been trained to a self-sufficient maturity, that you enter into a generous common life with those who have trained you, sharing all the good things that you have and experience.

GALATIANS 6:6 MSG

TAKING INVENTORY

> On the subject of sexual purity, what do you need to talk about with your daughter?

> What other dad/daughter-only topics would be good for you to talk with your girl about while taking a walk?

> While walking on the beach, be sure to talk about God's magnificent creation, and how we are the spiritual descendants of Abraham (who would be blessed with descendants as numerous as the sand on the seashore). What other spiritual teachable moments come to mind?

92. BE HER BIGGEST FAN

I would be hard-pressed if I were asked which of our girls' extracurricular pursuits through the years I enjoyed the most. I loved them all—elementary school dramas, junior high plays, high school musicals. (I even got to do the makeup for the Cat in the Hat and the Grinch in *Seussical the Musical*—I told you I was artsy!) Then there were all the sporting events, dance recitals, piano recitals, band concerts, and choral concerts. I could almost recite word for word the welcome speech Mrs. Santos gave every year at the Christmas concert.

As we hit the high school years, the amount of time invested—and money—escalated. "Just because the high school musical is performed five times, does that mean we have to attend *all five* times?" I asked my wife.

"Absolutely!" she responded.

"But, we've already paid a costume fee, and our name is on the back of the program as a 'silver patron,'" I snapped back.

"So. . .your point?" she questioned.

A smart man knows when he's got nothing more to say. So, with checkbook in hand, I trotted off to the theater box office to purchase multiple tickets for friends and family to *multiple* shows.

And I loved every minute of it. Especially when my girls looked out to cast a quick grin our way because they knew where we were sitting—where we were *always* sitting. I sat through *Pirates of Penzance, Les Miz, Brigadoon, The Wiz, A Midsummer Night's Dream, Twelfth Night, The Tempest, J.B.,* and other strange and wonderful shows. . .and I wouldn't trade it for the world.

Then we graduated to *a cappella* concerts performed by an all-girl ensemble, the Miami Misfitz, in an old, acoustically pleasing venue. Our younger daughter has a beautiful voice and an even more beautiful smile. I loved it when she glanced our way with a slight nod. I can't imagine not being there, or not giving her flowers at the end of her performance!

A WORD FROM THE WORD

May the LORD richly bless both you and your children.
PSALM 115:14 NLT

TAKING INVENTORY

> What are some of your daughter's events you've enjoyed the most?

> If you had it to do all over again, what opportunity would you not miss?

> You can offer your daughter the blessing of presence, just by being there. How else can you bless her immediately after her performances?

93. BE COOL AROUND HER GUY FRIENDS

My younger daughter has always had some close "guy friends." She never cared much for the "chick drama" that rears its ugly head in the junior high and high school years—and beyond. For that, I'm very grateful. When our daughter got to college, my wife and I really liked the fact that she had two very good guy friends who could protect her—were she to need it! They also had cars—which she did not—so she got frequent lifts to Walmart, the grocery store, and the outlet malls. In return, she'd sometimes cook for them—and they were all about that. They attended her music concerts. In fact, I'd venture to say they are in nearly every one of the post-concert photos we have. To a casual observer, they might look like part of the family. We have joked about the fact that these two dudes should be bridesmaids at her upcoming wedding.

One of them used to come to the house to sing and play guitar and piano with her. He once made the comment, "It's too bad you don't have a brother, because your dad is so cool. I'm sure your brother would have been awesome!"

My daughter responded, "What am I? Chopped liver?" I think he somehow managed to backtrack and smooth things over with her. Regardless, what he said made my week. The fact that I don't have any boys of my own is probably one of the reasons I love having her guy friends over. I can talk sports with them. I can share my man cave with them, my own little testosterone retreat from the estrogen poisoning that is my life. (Hey, I have a schnauzer, and even she's a girl!)

Having the same guy around your house all the time, and letting him sleep on your couch—because he's head over heels in love with your daughter—might not be a good thing. But having lots of her guy friends over is positive. So just be yourself around them. They may be into sports, music, girls, or artsy pursuits—hopefully you'll find something in common with them. Buy them a meal every now and then (especially if they are poor college kids!) Watch some hoops with them. But don't judge their music. And don't make any comments about their hair (or lack of it), their clothes, their cars, or their political views. Take your cues from your daughter concerning what you can talk about. If you pass the test, and they think you're cool enough, they might even invite you into their fantasy football league. How cool would that be?

A WORD FROM THE WORD

Friends love through all kinds of weather,
and families stick together in all kinds of trouble.
PROVERBS 17:17 MSG

TAKING INVENTORY

> How have you helped your daughter navigate through chick drama?

> What are some things you have in common with your daughter's guy friends?

> By hanging around with her guy friends when you are invited in, what life lessons are you teaching your daughter?

94. LOOK FOR COMMON GROUND

Do you have something unique that you share with your daughter? Use it to your advantage—and hers! Maybe it's the fact that you have the same color hair or eyes, or you both wear glasses. Maybe you both have six toes on one foot. Maybe you're both firstborns, or both of you are "the baby in the family."

I share a special bond with my younger daughter because we're both the youngest kid in our families. As she was trying to navigate through those gawky pre-teen years (neither of our girls knew they even *had* a gawky stage until years later), there were times when knowing she wasn't the only one to ever get a raw deal, or the shaft, helped her. Often, just by relating some of my more embarrassing moments to her, I got a laugh out of her—and, suddenly her lot in life didn't seem so bad. Her older sister couldn't hold a candle to some of the things my older brother did to me!

As she became a teenager, it didn't necessarily help her to know I had gone through something similar, because by then she was convinced I was a geek throughout my junior high and senior high teen years—which is basically true. Geek or not, look for the common ground to encourage your girl the best way you know how. It might seem like something small to you at the time, but it could be huge in her world.

Be joyful. Grow to maturity. Encourage each other. Live in harmony and peace. Then the God of love and peace will be with you.
2 Corinthians 13:11 nlt

TAKING INVENTORY

> What are at least five things you have in common with your daughter?

> How can you use those areas to encourage her?

> What are some positive traits you see in your daughter that you don't have? Praise her for those.

95. TAKE HER GOLFING

Besides teaching your daughter how to drive a car, nothing may try your patience more than teaching her how to hit a golf ball. Somewhere during my daughters' junior high years, I tried to convince them to take up golf, suggesting it would be a great way to earn a college scholarship. My efforts were in vain—they simply were not interested. They had seen me fall asleep on many a lazy Sunday afternoon to the pleasant and quiet commentary of a PGA broadcast, and probably deduced that the sport couldn't be very exciting.

And then something unexpected happened in their late high school and early college years. Suddenly, both girls became interested in golf. I don't know if it was because they had enjoyed some family rounds of miniature golf, just wanted to do something with me because I was paying, or had suddenly taken notice of the cute outfits the women on the LPGA circuit were wearing. I informed them that we would first need to head out to a driving range in order to learn the game before getting on an actual golf course. (I highly recommend this option over your backyard—unless a yard full of divots complements the patio décor.)

If you choose to follow my advice and take your daughter to a driving range, be prepared to stay for a while. You'll be dispensing the basics—the correct grip, stance, backswing, follow-through, and how to properly address the ball—as well as explaining the differences between woods, irons, wedges, and the putter. . .followed by lots of swings and misses, giggles, and embarrassment. If your girl has played other sports, like softball, she may already have decent hand-eye coordination—and that will definitely be to her advantage. Keep assuring her that everybody has to start somewhere, and many people on the driving range have been in the same place she is—even if that's not true!

Once she can hit a ball decently (or as inconsistently as you still hit it), get her out on a par 3 course. She'll love picking out shoes and cute clothes to wear. Remind her that the better she looks the more other people will expect out of her golf game. Prior to playing a round, you'll explain the meaning of "fore" and why she should be quiet when other people are hitting. Be sure to pack an extra measure of patience in your bag before you put it in the trunk of your car. Meanwhile, your daughter will probably be more concerned with how cute looks in her golf attire than learning the indispensable nuggets of wisdom you are seeking to impart. And even after a bad day on the golf course, it can all be redeemed by stopping for soft-serve ice cream at the local Whippy Dip.

A WORD FROM THE WORD

Give yourselves to disciplined instruction;
open your ears to tested knowledge.
PROVERBS 23:12 MSG

TAKING INVENTORY

> If your sport is not golf, what sport could you teach your daughter how to play?

> By teaching her this sport, what life lessons are you passing on to her?

> What other things can you teach your daughter that will be an asset to your relationship as she grows older?

> DARN, SHE'S BASICALLY A WOMAN <

96. CREATE A SAFE ZONE FOR COMMUNICATING THE HARD THINGS

Your daughter needs a safety net where she can tell you *absolutely anything*, because she trusts you, without fearing rejection or overreaction. This is bigger than simply being a good listener, although it certainly is built on that foundation. It means not reacting visibly when she tells you she dented your car. It means keeping your temper when she tells you she failed a class or got suspended. It means allowing her to finish her comments without interruption when she tells you about the boy who pressed her to get physical on their second date. (You'll want her to keep talking long enough to get his address so you can drive to his house with a shotgun and a shovel.) Just joking.

Your daughter will talk to her mom about some things, her sister, brother, or friends about others, but when it comes to the big issues, she needs *you*. A friend in college expressed her need for this long before I was even thinking about marriage, much less being a dad. She said, "When I want the advice of a brother, I go to your roommate; but when I want the advice of a father, I come to you." That made such a deep impression on me because I had never thought of myself in that role with girls who were my own age. But my friend had figured out, even at the age of nineteen, that when the stakes were high, she needed *safety* and *acceptance* without losing sight of the bigger picture of *responsibility* and *action*. Whoever else may comfort your daughter, *you* will be her safe harbor and guide if you maintain a safe relationship.

He found him in a desert land,
And in the howling waste of a wilderness;
He encircled him, He cared for him,
He guarded him as the pupil of His eye.

DEUTERONOMY 32:10

OUR TRANSLATION

> God seeks us out to protect us, to cover us, to give us a safe place. We can do that for our children and it will give them a picture of God that mere words will never accomplish.

97. LEARN TO ACCEPT DEFEAT

At some point during their high school years, my daughters surpassed my knowledge in the field of mathematics. I never got past pre-calc. My younger daughter, on the other hand, is now teaching calculus in high school. If she happens to be home when I pull out the sudoku puzzle in the local section of the newspaper, a fight ensues regarding who will get to work the puzzle first. If it's on a Thursday or Friday, I simply let her have it without a struggle, as the sudokus get progressively harder the deeper you go into the week. This is just one example of how I have learned to accept defeat.

I tell people all the time that one of the reasons I do the sudoku, cryptoquip, and crossword puzzles in the paper every day is that I am hoping to avoid Alzheimer's disease. It's also one of the reasons I watch *Jeopardy* as often as I can. My nemesis at home is my elder daughter. On certain nights, when the categories consist of the Old Testament, Disco Acts of the '70s, Super Bowl Foods, and Rhyme Time, I own the game. But if Double Jeopardy consists of Children's Lit, Pop Music, Shakespeare, and Fads of the '90s, I'm toast. On those nights, I wonder what else I should be accomplishing. But before I sneak off, my daughter is onto my ploy and the match is on—however feeble my performance might be. If it's Teen Week or College Week on *Jeopardy*, I might as well throw in the towel before Alex sends us off to our first commercial break.

The lesson? She loves beating me. I don't know where she learned to be so competitive; it must have come from her mother's side! My guess is that your daughter will eventually discover some things she is better at than you are. It may come now, it may come later. . .but it will come. Your job will be to learn how to lose and still keep smiling.

Because I'm a writer and an editor, my wife refuses to play any word games with me. I don't understand this. She's a dental hygienist, but I still go to the dentist every six months, don't I? My daughter, however, will play Scrabble and our new favorite game, Bananagrams, with me. I am very good at bluffing when a word I've placed on the board will not be found in the dictionary—and, generally speaking, she's still afraid to challenge me. Therefore, I still own her in these games—most of the time. On those rare nights when she crushes me in *Jeopardy* and then adds salt to the wound by besting me in Scrabble, I smile outwardly, attempt to accept my defeat graciously, and then saunter off to bed, thanking God for giving me such brilliant daughters.

A WORD FROM THE WORD

A sterling reputation is better than striking it rich;
a gracious spirit is better than money in the bank.
PROVERBS 22:1 MSG

LORD, be gracious to us; we long for you. Be our strength
every morning, our salvation in time of distress.
ISAIAH 33:2 NIV

TAKING INVENTORY

> What are some things at which your daughter is better than you are?

> By showing you have the ability to lose with grace, what are you telling your daughter about yourself?

> What games provide the most fertile ground for competition between the two of you?

98. TAKE HER SHOPPING FOR HER FIRST CAR

I'm a big believer in not purchasing your daughter's first car for her; rather, let her get a sense of the magnitude of the responsibility by having her pay for all—or most of it—herself. She will appreciate her first car so much more because she will see it as *her* investment—not yours.

Neither one of our girls had her own car in high school—they drove one of ours. And they both had the benefit of going to a college that has a great bus system to get them around campus and to the local Kroger. They've each had friends who had their own cars, so they could always get a lift when needed. So, it wasn't until our eldest graduated from college, got a full-time job, and had saved up some money before she was ready to go car shopping. I offered some guidance, and she got some quality advice from other males in the family who know cars—but she did the homework herself. She researched makes and models, and which dealerships were offering discounts, rebates, etc. She checked dealership websites, seeing what was available where.

When we went car shopping, she did most of the talking with sales managers and sales reps. I chimed in a few germane comments here and there, but mostly tried to be a silent support. She did the test driving. . .and really didn't need the salesman's tutorial for OnStar. We called our insurance provider together, but I let her walk through the details on the phone, and offered my support in the background. There were a few stressful moments along the way for her—but she learned some great lessons that will benefit her for the rest of her life. Now she's making the payments every month, is a little more motivated to help wash the cars on Sunday afternoons, and a bit more concerned about all the miles she is putting on her wheels on the way to and from work. But she is proud of her first big investment and her beautiful blue Malibu!

TAKING INVENTORY

> What are some benefits and drawbacks to your daughter's not having a car to drive until after high school?

> What signs of responsibility will you look for in your daughter so that you will know she is ready for her first car?

> What are some practical ways you can show her your support?

99. LET HER EDIT YOUR BOOK

I realize this may be a long shot, because not many men write things—and especially things their daughters would be interested in. Most men barely read (which is what makes you so special for reading this book). If you are the writing or journaling type, it's an amazing experience to invite your daughter into that part of your world. It allows her to see how you think when you are making a point of putting it on paper. And asking for her input into your writing tells her she is intellectually valuable.

It might also help you eliminate mistakes, since the memory bank in the female mind is, generally speaking, more accurate than our own. You might even learn something. Imagine!

It also gives you a great opportunity to express appreciation when you find out she has something to say. Even if she passes on the invitation to mark up your manuscript, there's no way she'll miss out on the vote of confidence from her dad.

TAKING INVENTORY

> Because most dads (including Dale and me) will spend more time with a remote in their hands than a pen, let me expand on the principle of asking for your daughter's input on something that's close to your heart. Anything that you would *never dream* of asking your daughter's opinion about is fair game. For example . . .

> your fantasy football picks

> your next fishing getaway

> what to plant in the garden

> what to do with your tax refund

In other words, anything that you handle in a semi-autonomous way can become an occasion to expand her understanding (and yours).

100. GET HER READY FOR THE REAL WORLD

There's no substitute for getting your daughter ready for the real world like. . .throwing her out into the real world. It's sort of like the "practical ministries" class I had in college. It didn't seem very *practical* while I was sitting in the classroom listening to less-than-engaging lectures and dreaming of playing basketball or what I was going to eat for lunch in the cafeteria. It wasn't practical until I was thrust into my first job and suddenly needed to know some of that stuff.

I tried to instill some money management principles into the lives of my daughters; basic things such as, "Take in more than you spend," and, "You can't buy something with a check if you don't have the money in the bank." Not rocket science. But it really wasn't until they were out of college, and trying to figure out how much of their paychecks would go to things like health insurance, car insurance, car payments, groceries, entertainment, gifts, etc., that they were ready to listen. And then perhaps only because they wanted to know if they'd have enough money saved for an upcoming trip to Europe.

We have a saying we use whenever we see a young adult who seems clueless about making ends meet, or someone in college who's been given a free ride by her parents: "She's not living in the real world." My advice is to do whatever you can to help your daughters see the big picture: God owns everything, and we are merely stewards of what he gives us. And we need to be *good* stewards. Without necessarily letting your daughter see the nitty-gritty of the financial pressures you've faced, let her see your dependence on God most of all. Try to counteract what she is fed by the world by teaching her the evils of credit cards and "minimum payments."

My experience is that you will suddenly become smart in this area when your daughter reaches her twenties. If you've planted the right seeds, some of your nuggets of wisdom will start to make sense to her. At the same time, you'll come to the realization that she has already learned how to be a professional shopper and consumer because of her mother's "real world training."

A WORD FROM THE WORD

Foolish dreamers live in a world of illusion;
wise realists plant their feet on the ground.
PROVERBS 14:18 MSG

Committed and persistent work pays off;
get-rich-quick schemes are ripoffs.
PROVERBS 28:20 MSG

TAKING INVENTORY

> What are some things you didn't know before you left home and set off into the great big world?

> What are the top ten things you'd like your daughter to know before you launch her into the real world?

> What financial principles would you like to instill in her?

101. HELP HER MOVE IN

As parents, our job is ultimately to give our kids all the necessary tools they will need to survive in the real world—then release them into their future, and let them go with our blessings. Nobody ever said it would be easy—but that's our task. Sometimes, I envision this task as similar to that of the seals off the coast of South Africa, who raise their pups only to see many of them devoured by Great White sharks lurking offshore. Have you ever watched Shark Week on the Discovery Channel? *Not pretty*—unless, of course, you're a fan of sharks.

Over the course of six years, my wife and I moved one or both of our daughters to college every August. The first year we took our eldest to Miami University, we packed up everything we thought she'd need, including adaptors for all manner of electronica. She took *way* more clothes than necessary (considering it was still over 90 degrees most days, and she wouldn't be needing the winter coat for quite a while). My wife and the mother of our daughter's roommate helped the girls unpack, made their beds, and debated whether it would be better to go bunk style, or side by side (thus losing valuable floor space in a dorm room about the size of an average closet).

Sweating profusely after carrying all the boxes in from the car, I let the women do their thing, while I headed for the porch swing and chilled with a bottle of water. That's when I began to notice a few sharks lurking about (some of whom would even be in my daughter's dorm—which was coed). There were other "sharks," as well. . .things that could deter her from her studies, distractions of all sorts, being swept up into a sea of thousands, the fear of losing her identity and individuality, and even her faith. I wondered how my "baby seal" would fare in these cold waters so far from home. (Okay, it was only a forty-five-minute drive from our house, but that first year it seemed farther than that.)

My quiet reflections were interrupted when I was informed that we would be heading to the local Walmart. "But I thought we brought everything from home already. What more could she possibly need?"

I soon learned that every year would include this same trip to Walmart, for whatever it was we'd forgotten or had never fathomed she could need. Inevitably, we'd see a raft of other feverishly shopping college kids and parents—snapping up window fans, big-screen TVs, ramen noodles, backpacks, door mirrors, adaptors, photo frames. . .as if these were the last to be had in the developed world. It's quite a ritual to behold.

As the fathers were busy calculating in their heads how much this trip—and the whole four years' experience—was going to cost them, the moms were checking off "necessary" items on the list for their prince or princess. As the years progressed and our girls moved off campus, *IKEA* became a code word for putting together furniture (or anything else) with minimal tools and no directions in English—only pictures.

Suffice to say, each year the process of moving in got a little easier. But after dropping the girls off at their dorm, or house, or apartment, I always found myself wiping away a tear or two as my wife and I drove off into the sunset. In our wake, the sharks still swam about. God help our baby seals.

TAKING INVENTORY

> What "sharks" are lurking about for your daughter as she becomes an adult?

> What practical things can you do to prepare her to navigate the icy waters with the sharks?

> Since more is often "caught than taught," what do you hope your daughter has caught from you that will serve her well for the rest of her life?

ABOUT THE AUTHORS

Jess MacCallum is president of Professional Printers, Inc. in Columbia, South Carolina. Author of two previous books, he is father of two daughters and a son.

Dale Reeves is pastor of adult discipleship for Christ's Church at Mason, Ohio. He and his wife have two grown daughters.